Machine Quilting

The basics & beyond

by Lynn Witzenburg

Landauer Books

Machine Quilting
The basics & beyond
by Lynn Witzenburg

Copyright © 2008 by Landauer Corporation

This book was designed, produced,
and published by Landauer Books
A division of Landauer Corporation
3100 101st Street, Urbandale, Iowa 50322
www.landauercorp.com   800/557-2144

President/Publisher: Jeramy Lanigan Landauer
Director of Sales & Operations: Kitty Jacobson
Editor: Jane Townswick
Managing Editor: Jeri Simon
Art Director: Laurel Albright
Technical Editor: Rhonda Matus
Technical Illustrator: Linda Bender
Photographer: Craig Anderson

ISBN 13: 978-0-9793711-3-4
ISBN 10: 0-9793711-3-9

This book is printed on acid-free paper.
Printed in China

10 9 8 7 6 5 4 3 2 1

Machine Quilting, The basics & beyond
Library of Congress Control Number: 2007941432

Introduction

I have been machine quilting professionally since 1996. While recovering from repetitive stress injuries to both of my arms caused from typing on computers for too many years, I realized that I would never be able to hand quilt again. I had done some machine quilting, and knew that was the only way my quilt tops would ever progress. I had time on my hands because our boys were in school and I could no longer work in the computer field. After seeing my quilts, friends began asking if I would quilt tops for them which was great because I wanted to fill the empty hours of my days. Soon the requests were increasing and I had a bright idea to start charging for my time. My machine quilting business was born. Within a few years I was teaching at a local quilt shop and began receiving requests for lectures and trunk shows from guilds in the area.

Teaching is my favorite thing to do! I have learned so much from my students over the years. Things that came very easy to me are not always easy for others. Learning this has helped me to see different ways to approach the many things that cause frustration for others. I like to share all the mistakes, and things I've learned from those mistakes so others can move right past those pitfalls. "**There are no rules**" is my mantra, and if there are, there must be a way to break them! Question every rule; find the reason why if there is one. People get so caught up in what they were told was a 'rule' that they forget to experiment and grow from the discoveries. Quilting is constantly evolving with new ideas, techniques and tools, some good, some not so good. Keeping an open mind is the best approach.

Another piece of advice I've given over and over that seems to help many students is to quilt that top you're stuck on and move on to the next. So many students bring quilt tops to me for advice on how to quilt them but are just frozen when thinking about taking the first stitch. If you just do your best on each quilt top you quilt and move on to the next, you'll be amazed at your own progress. Adjust your attitude to have the determination to be able to say, "I made this quilt from start to finish." If you're like the students and former customers I've taught, you'll love doing your own quilting. Plus, you'll have that much more money to buy fabric!

I'd like to say a special thank you to my husband, Ray, who has always been my best friend and biggest supporter. He has everything to do with why I am who I am today. Also, a big thanks to our sons, Bruce and Adam, who turned the fact that I rarely cook into a family joke.

A very special thank you is due to my good friend, Connie Doern, owner of Creekside Quilting in Clive, IA for her generosity in loaning me a sewing machine and use of her classroom for several photos. She also gives me the opportunity to teach my machine quilting class regularly in her shop.

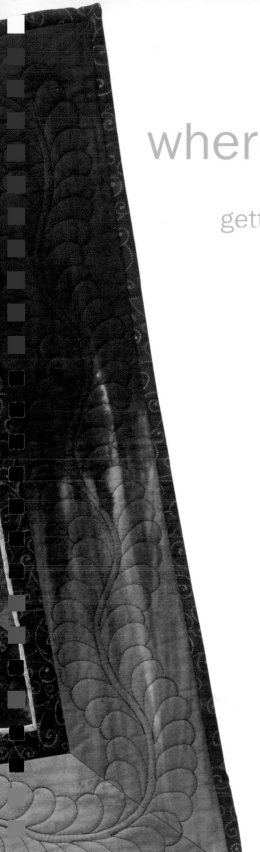

where to find it

getting started—basics & beyond

You'll find all the basics of machine quilting in the following chapters. I've included practice patterns that will help you build your skills and confidence before tackling a full-size project. Each chapter is presented in an easy format to guarantee your success. You'll find instructions for some of my favorite quilting projects. Each one includes a quilting diagram and suggestions on how to quilt your project to make it spectacular.

Lynn

Equipment & Supplies is a must first read. This information will assist you when selecting tools and supplies for your machine quilting projects. Most of the equipment and supplies will be familiar to experienced quilters. Experiment with different threads, needles, batting, and tools to discover what gives your project that extra something.

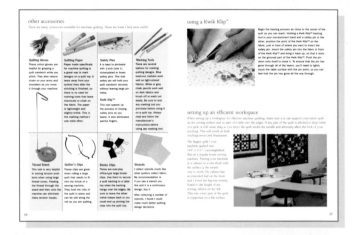

Preparing to Machine Quilt explains why it's important to keep a practice quilt beside your machine. Detailed photographs accompany each section and includes basic information you will use every time you begin to machine quilt your projects.
Learn the importance of:
• Adjusting your thread tension.
• Beginning and ending a line of stitching.
• Moving from one section of quilting to another.
• Bringing up the bobbin thread for great tension from the very first stitch.

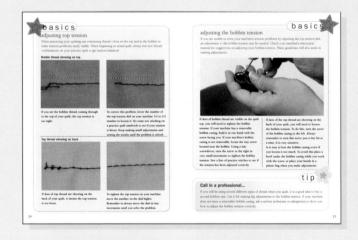

Techniques is packed with free-motion practice quilting patterns and suggestions. Each pattern is outlined with step-by-step directions and close-up photography. You'll learn how to turn your practice doodling into beautiful free-form feather designs, flowers, words, and much more.

You'll also find information about choosing stencils, adapting quilting motifs to fill spaces, Trapunto, and bobbin quilting. Plus, plenty of instruction on marking your quilting designs and using quilting paper.

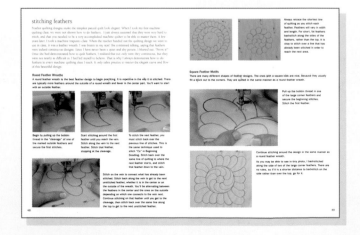

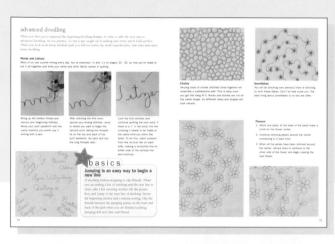

Basics can be found throughout the first chapters of the book. This information is highlighted in yellow and includes techniques that will be needed each time you begin a machine quilting project.

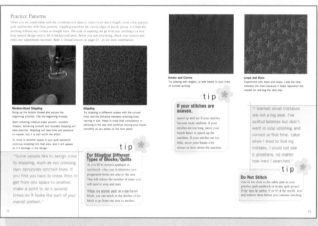

Tips offer helpful troubleshooting ideas to make you successful in your machine quilting adventure. They are not essential to the process, but are easy to identify with a blue background.

My personal, first-hand experiences and tips are highlighted in green.

Quilting a Full-size Quilt takes the fear out of quilting a large project on your sewing machine. You will see how easy it is to baste, roll, and free-motion quilt your project, no matter what size it is. Additional information on the type of stitching to use to enhance each block or appliqué area is provided, as well as the order in which to quilt for the best result.

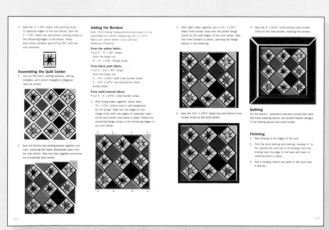

Projects encourages you to take everything you have learned to create your own masterpiece. Ten gorgeous projects in varying sizes and skill levels are showcased in the last chapter. Each includes complete instructions and step-by-step illustrations. Quilting options and diagrams will entice you to begin your own machine quilting journey.

equipment & supplies

Having the right tools will go a long way toward making any type of quilting task a success. As you read, remember I am sharing the tools that work for me. Keep your mind open to new sewing devices and quilting gadgets. Then you'll be able to decide which tools and equipment will work best for you.

equipment & supplies

The next few pages will give you information on products that will enhance your machine quilting experience. You should also ask friends, fellow guild members, and quilt shop employees about their favorite tools for machine quilting. This will help you decide which supplies to purchase to get started.

Sewing Machine Features

There is such a wide variety of sewing machines on the market today it can make your head spin trying to determine which features you need. Some older machines may not have a strong enough motor to effectively handle the multiple layers of a quilt sandwich when machine quilting. If you are planning to purchase a new machine, look for the listed features I find most important for machine quilting.

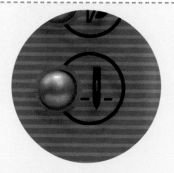

Needle Stop Down

This function allows the needle to stop in the down position when you stop sewing. You are able to stop stitching to clip threads, remove pins, or readjust the position of your hands and then continue quilting without shifting your quilt or breaking your line of stitches.

Half-Stitch Capability

On some machines, the foot pedal has the capability of taking a half stitch with a single tap of your heel or the touch of a button. This is helpful for bringing up the bobbin thread or raising the needle out of the fabric when you want to reposition the quilt sandwich.

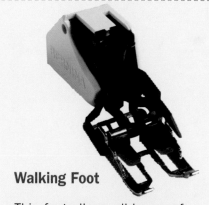

Walking Foot

This foot allows all layers of a quilt sandwich to move through the machine evenly as you stitch. Some of today's machines have a built-in walking foot, while it is an added accessory on other machines.

Free-Motion or Darning Foot

In addition to the walking foot, the main presser foot used in machine quilting is the free-motion foot. It may also be referred to as a darning foot. If you do not own one, it is well worth the investment. Purchase one compatible with the type and model of the sewing machine you own. A free-motion foot made of clear plastic allows better visibility when stitching backwards.

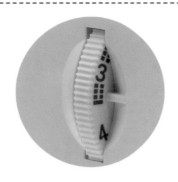

Tension Dial

All machines have a dial or knob which controls thread tension. It is best when located on the machine's top or side where it cannot easily be bumped.

Stitch Width & Length

The stitch width and length regulator is standard on sewing machines. You will use this feature when stitching in the ditch and using your walking foot.

When free-motion machine quilting you control the width and length of your stitches with the movement of your hands and will not be using this feature.

Feed Dogs

Feed dogs are raised (photo 1) for piecing, but should be lowered (photo 2) when free-motion stitching. This allows you to move your quilt smoothly under the needle. Some machines are equipped with a cover for the feed dogs.

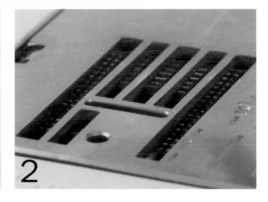

Wish List

Adjustable Presser Foot Pressure

On many new sewing machine models you can vary the pressure of the presser foot. This allows you to adjust the height of the presser foot in its lowered position to accommodate the loft of thicker quilts.

Extra-large Sewing Space

The space between the needle and the right side of the machine is referred to as the throat. This is the area through which you will move at least half of a quilt sandwich. On some of today's machines this space is extra large, allowing more room for maneuvering a quilt through the machine.

Knee Lift

This lever enables you to lift the presser foot with your knee and allows you to turn or move the quilt sandwich while keeping both hands on the fabric. This increases your stitching accuracy.

needles

The needles you choose for machine quilting are important in two ways. First, the life of your sewing machine depends on how hard the motor must work to push the needle through all the layers of a quilt sandwich. It is of paramount importance to use a very sharp needle as opposed to a universal or ballpoint needle. Second, balancing the thread tension is vital for achieving even stitching. You don't want dots of thread to pop through to the opposite side of your quilt. This is easier to accomplish when you use the right needle with the right thread.

When purchasing needles keep in mind the higher the number, the larger the needle. A size 80/12 needle is a medium size, which works for most quilts made with cotton fabric and cotton batting.

If your quilt is heavier, such as one made from flannel or denim, or it has many small patches with a lot of seam allowances, try using a size 90/14 needle. For a quilt featuring batiks on the front and back sides and a very light batting, a size 70/10 needle will suffice.

Though there is room for experimentation with various needle sizes, it is best to use the smallest needle possible for your project. This ensures that the holes made in the quilt sandwich will be as tiny as possible, and make it easier for the machine's motor to push the needle through the layers. I have narrowed the needle choices to five that have served me well for the various types of machine quilting I have done.

When using heavier threads such as 40-wt. and above the size of your needle should be at least 90/14.

Quilting Needles

Quilting needles typically come two sizes per pack 75/11 and 90/14. These have a very sharp point and are ideal for most quilting situations.

Sharps

The sharps are sold one size per pack but are available in several sizes. For a very sharp point, I like the 70/10 for light weight and batik projects.

Topstitch Needles

These needles are heavier needles with a larger eye. They are nice for heavier threads, such as 12-wt. cotton. The larger eye makes it easier to thread and reduces drag as the thread goes through the eye.

Jeans Needles

Jeans needles are for very heavy duty fabrics such as denim or flannel.

Metallic Needles

These are made to be used with metallic thread, which can add a nice sparkle to any quilt. If you don't use a metallic needle in conjunction with a metallic thread, you will find that the thread breaks frequently due to the friction that builds up when the metal in the thread rubs against the metal needle, resulting in high temperatures. Metallic needles have a large eye that is coated with Teflon to reduce this buildup of heat.

tip

Thread breaking

One of the most common ways to tell if the eye in your needle is too small for the size of your thread is that when you are sewing the thread will fray and/or break.

threads

There are no rules when it comes to thread. Experimenting with new types of thread is fun and can change the entire look of the quilt.

A few things to remember about thread:

Using a similar weight of thread on top and in the bobbin is usually the easiest way to balance the tension.

The weight/gauge of the thread differs between thread manufacturers. Use your best judgment to determine if two different threads are similar in weight.

When using a heavy thread on top, a lightweight cotton or polyester thread in the bobbin can help balance the tension. Be prepared to make tension adjustments.

Threads that work well in one sewing machine may be a disaster in another. Always experiment on a practice sandwich when trying new thread combinations.

When experimenting with new threads, check the needle you are using. Sometimes just changing the size or type of needle can make a difference in the stitches.

If you are experiencing constant thread breakage and have ruled out all other potential problems, change to another spool of the same type and color of thread. This will sometimes solve the problem.

Stay away from the bargain bins of thread for piecing or machine quilting. You'll get what you pay for.

Experiment—be open to new types and colors of thread. If you're uncertain as to what needle to use, check with the manufacturer or just experiment. You'll be amazed at your own creativity.

> "I use a wide array of thread when machine quilting. I love all the variegated threads which can be cotton, polyester or rayon. They add a new dimension to any quilt."
>
> **tip**

I've discovered

When using metallic thread, instead of putting it on the spool holder I thread it through a thread stand. By laying the spool loose on the base of the thread stand, it feeds without any tension or pulling and breaks less frequently.

batting choices

There are many types of batting available and choosing the right one for your quilt can be confusing. Knowing the basic aspects of different types of batting will help you make an informed decision. The loft, or thickness, of the batting should be considered. A thicker batting creates more bulk in the sewing machine. The type of thread can also be a factor when choosing batting. For a thread heavier than 50-weight, a thicker batting can make it easier to balance your thread tension. Below are the types of batting I use most often and why.

- **Mountain Mist® Cream Rose/White Rose**

    This batting is 100 percent cotton and is very soft and thin. It gives a quilt an antique, draping look, and a soft feel.

- **Mountain Mist® Blue Ribbon or Completely Cotton**

    These battings are 100 percent cotton and feel slightly heavier than the Cream Rose and White Rose batts but are approximately the same weight per square yard. The difference is in the manufacturing method. These are both very soft and a good choice if you are using heavier threads. These batts were used in many of the samples and projects in this book.

- **Warm and Natural®/Warm and White®**

    I like the warmth and strength of these battings. Either is great for a bed quilt or quilted jackets. However, if your quilt will be folded for long periods of time you will want to choose a different batting.

Fold lines tend to stay more pronounced in this batting and projects must be steamed to hang or lie flat. Although once the quilt has been washed a few time the folds are no longer a problem.

- **Quilters Dream**

    This batting is available in different levels of loft. The lowest, or Request loft, is the type I have used most often for machine quilting. It is a very thin, soft, 100 percent cotton batting, which gives a nice antique look and drapes nicely. It is also a good choice for quilt tops that are already heavy and don't need extra weight. If you plan to use heavier thread, the Select loft may be a better choice.

- **Hobbs Heirloom® Wool**

    Wool is much warmer than cotton. This thin batting has just enough loft to show off your machine quilting stitches. This is a favorite for many of my customers. This batting is machine washable and can be dried in the dryer.

Use your own judgement

Battings have directions on the side of the package with recommendations for size of non-quilted spaces between quilting lines. You can test your batting by trying to pull it apart at one edge. If it separates easily, the non-quilted areas in your quilt will need to be no more than 2 to 3-inches apart. If it does not pull apart easily, then you can leave larger unquilted areas.

"To me a quilt is not really a quilt unless it can be machine washed and dried. Most of the time the quilting shows up better after the quilt has been laundered. A little bit of shrinkage is a good thing.

Always check the recommendations on the batting package for laundering your finished quilt."

sewing machine maintenance

Keeping your sewing machine cleaned and oiled is important for doing beautiful machine quilting. Regular maintenance will keep your machine running more efficiently, resulting in better tension balance, a longer motor life, and more beautiful quilts.

Find a good sewing machine technician and take your machine in for servicing at least once a year. Look for someone who is willing to explain the best way to clean and oil your machine between service calls. I routinely clean and oil my machine after every other bobbin. If I'm using a cotton thread that creates more lint, I clean it after every bobbin. I also have it serviced on a regular basis so the tension is always perfect.

other accessories

There are many accessories available for machine quilting. These are some I find most useful.

Quilting Gloves

These cotton gloves are helpful for gripping a quilt sandwich while you stitch. They also reduce strain on your arms and shoulders as you move it through your machine.

Quilting Paper

Paper made specifically for machine quilting is a great way to mark designs on a quilt top. It tears away from your quilted lines after the stitching is finished, so there is no need for marking tools that leave chemicals or chalk on the fabric. The paper is lightweight and slightly brittle. This is the marking method I use most often.

Safety Pins

It is best to pin-baste with 1-inch (size 1) nickel-plated or brass safety pins. This size safety pin will hold your quilt sandwich securely without leaving large pin holes.

Kwik Klip™

This tool speeds up the process of closing safety pins as you baste. It also eliminates painful fingers.

Marking Tools

There are several options for marking quilting designs. Blue wash-out markers work well on light-colored fabrics. White or grey chalk pencils work well on dark fabrics and brush off or wash out easily. Be sure to test any marking tool you purchase before using it on a quilt top. Always read and follow the manufacturer's instructions before using any marking tool.

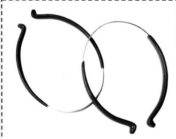

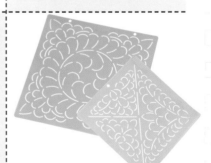

Thread Stand

This tool is very helpful in solving tension problems when using large thread cones. Feeding the thread through the stand and then onto the machine can eliminate many tension issues.

Quilter's Clips

These clips are great when rolling a large quilt that needs to fit into the throat of a sewing machine. They hold the rolls of the quilt in place and can be slid along the roll as you are quilting.

Binder Clips

These are everyday office-type large binder clips. Use them to secure a quilt backing to a table top when the backing hangs over the edges. Be sure to leave the silver metal clasps back or you could end up pinning the clips into the quilt top.

Stencils

I collect stencils much like other quilters collect fabric. My recommendation is if you see a stencil you like and it is a continuous design, buy it.

After collecting a number of stencils, I found I could make much better quilting design decisions.

using a Kwik Klip™

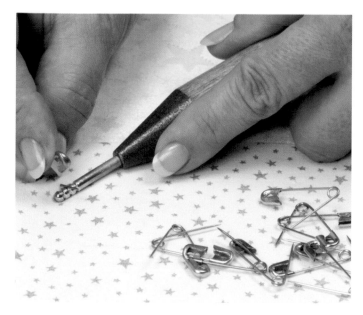

Begin the basting process as close to the center of the quilt as you can reach. Holding a Kwik Klip™ basting tool in your non-dominant hand and a safety pin in the other, position the point of the Kwik Klip™ on the fabric, just in front of where you want to insert the safety pin. Insert the safety pin into the fabric in front of the Kwik Klip™ and bring it back up, so that it rests on the grooved part of the Kwik Klip™. Push the pin down onto itself to close it. To ensure that the pin has gone through all of the layers, you'll need to lightly touch the table surface with the pin point, so you can feel that the pin has gone all the way through.

setting up an efficient workspace

When setting up a workspace for effective machine quilting, make sure you can support your entire quilt on the sewing surface and no part of it falls over the edges. If any part of the quilt is allowed to drop while you quilt, it will cause drag as you move the quilt under the needle and adversely affect the look of your stitching. This will result in both stitching errors and frustration.

The largest quilt I ever machine quilted was 144" x 111". I accomplished this on a regular home sewing machine. Putting your machine in a cabinet so it sets flush with the surface is the easiest way to work. My cabinet has an extended leaf on the front and I lower my big-top ironing board to the height of my sewing cabinet on my left. This way every part of the quilt is supported on a flat surface.

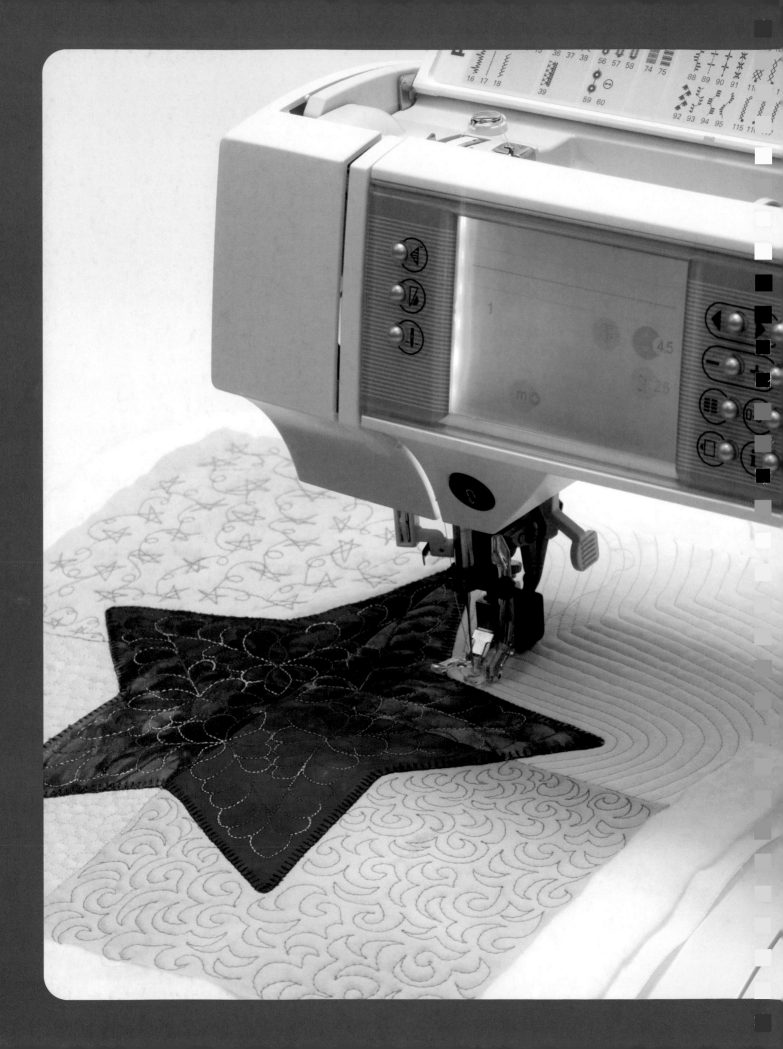

preparing to machine quilt

I approach machine quilting with a 'no rules, anything goes' philosophy. However, there are some basic steps that I follow whenever I begin a project. Learn the basics and then let your ideas and imagination flow.

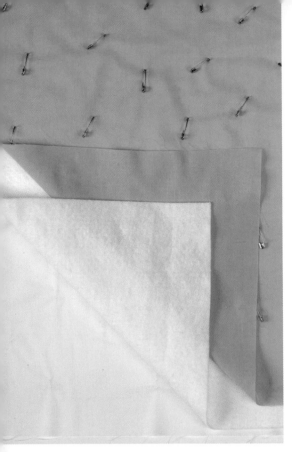

building a practice quilt sandwich

A practice quilt sandwich can be any size as long as the back is larger than the top. I recommend a 22" x 22" piece of muslin for the back and a 20" x 20" piece of muslin for the top. The batting needs to be larger than the top so anything 21" x 21" or larger will work. Using a lower loft batting will make things easier because there will be less bulk under the needle. Muslin or any other plain cotton fabric will work for the top and back. The color thread you choose should contrast with the fabric.

Press both pieces of fabric flat. Lay the backing fabric on a table top and tape the four corners of the fabric to the table with masking tape. **The fabric should be taut, not stretched**. Add one more piece of tape to each side.

Smooth the batting over the backing. There is no need to tape it down. Smooth the quilt top over the batting. There should be backing and batting extending out from under the top piece on all four sides.

Using your Kwik Klip™, insert safety pins in random order across the quilt top. Be sure to catch the backing, batting, and top with the pins. When you place your closed fist on the quilt top, you should be able to feel one or two pins, if not add a few more. You don't need any more pins than one or two per fist size especially on a quilt top this small. Once all the pins are in, remove the tape, and you are ready to start practicing.

 tip

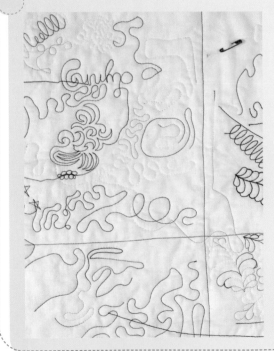

Always keep a practice quilt sandwich

Make it a habit to keep a practice quilt sandwich near your sewing machine, so you can test the way various threads react when you start a line of stitching. Different threads require different levels of securing in order to keep them from unraveling. For example, cotton threads are often the easiest to secure, because the cotton fibers of the thread mesh together easily with the fibers of the cotton fabric. Other threads, such as polyester and rayon, are more slippery and usually require taking a couple of extra stitches to secure. Metallic threads can be even more challenging and require extra locking stitches at the beginning of your line of quilting.

A practice quilt is a smart way to test your thread tension before beginning any project.

bringing up the bobbin thread

Before you begin any type of machine quilting, you will need to bring the bobbin thread up to the top of the quilt sandwich.

Lower the feed dogs on your sewing machine and lift the free-motion foot. Place the practice quilt sandwich under the foot where you want to begin quilting. Holding the top thread securely in your left hand, lower the needle into the quilt sandwich. On some machines this can be done with a single heel tap on the foot pedal or the touch of a button.

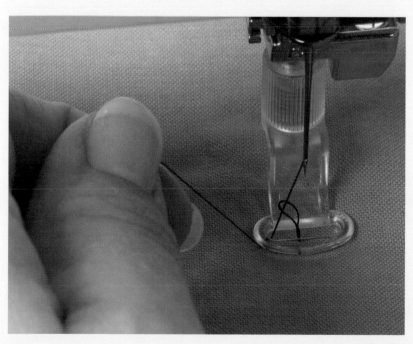

Lower the foot and take one stitch. The bobbin thread should pop up. If it doesn't, try again. It may help to take the first stitch with the foot raised, or to start in a different place on the quilt sandwich. Hold both the top and bobbin threads when taking your first few stitches.

beginning and ending a line of stitching

When beginning a line of machine quilting stitches, the threads of the first few stitches need to be secured, so they won't come undone. The visibility of the stitches should be as minimal as possible.

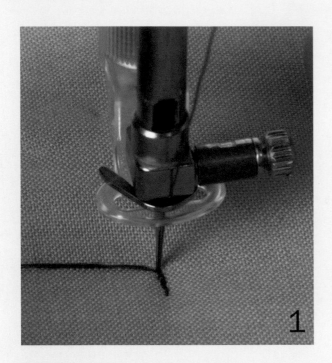

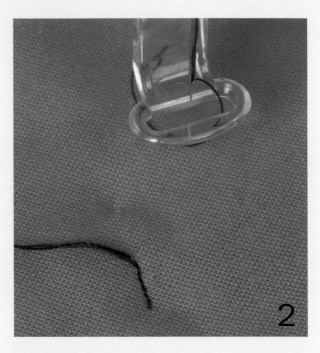

Method #1

One way to secure the beginning line of stitching is to lower the presser foot while holding the top and bobbin threads in your left hand. Take two or three stitches forward, then stitch backward over these same stitches, and forward again. The goal is to have as small a build-up of stitches visible as possible. Clip the beginning threads, so they do not become tangled in the subsequent stitches.

Method #2

Another way to secure a line of stitching is to take five or six very small stitches at the beginning. Make these stitches as small as possible, while still moving forward.

Securing the ending line of machine quilting stitches is the same as beginning. Sew backward over two or three stitches or take five or six very small stitches to end. If you choose the latter method, remember to stop your line of regular quilting stitches just short of the ending point to leave room for the small stitches.

thread tension

The top thread and the bobbin thread on your machine should lock somewhere in the center of your quilt sandwich with each stitch. This may mean adjusting the thread tension on your machine. It may seem a bit intimidating if you have not done it before. Read through the following guidelines and tips to achieve perfectly balanced quilting stitches.

Make only tiny adjustments to the top tension dial.
Do not roll the tension dial on your machine. It is very sensitive and often small changes are all that is needed to correct the tension. Take time to test the tension by stitching on a practice quilt sandwich after each adjustment. Evaluate your results and then go back and make further small changes, if necessary, until your stitches look perfect.

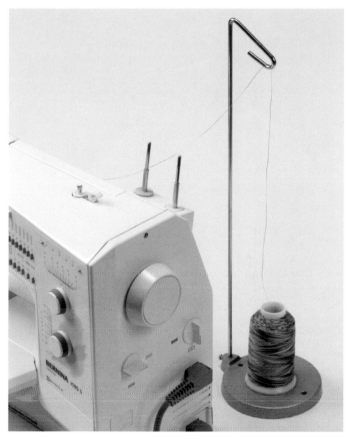

Thread the top thread through a thread stand.
This inexpensive tool is extremely helpful when using large thread cones. It will also help eliminate thread tension problems. Set the thread cone or spool on the metal post and thread it through the loop at the top and the normal threading route on your sewing machine. This creates less pull as the machine takes the thread from the spool, resulting in more even stitch tension.

tip

Thread ages

so keep in mind that threads from older spools may tend to break more often. Try a newer spool to see if the problem goes away. Storing thread in plastic bags in the freezer keeps it from aging as quickly.

basics

adjusting top tension

When practicing your quilting use contrasting thread colors on the top and in the bobbin to make tension problems easily visible. When beginning an actual quilt, always test new thread combinations on your practice quilt to get tension balanced.

Bobbin thread showing on top

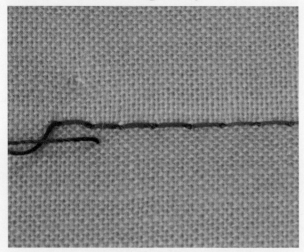

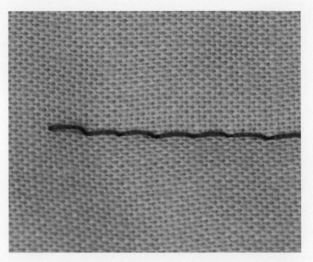

If you see the bobbin thread coming through to the top of your quilt, the top tension is too tight.

To correct this problem, lower the number of the top tension dial on your machine 1/4 to 1/2 number to loosen it. Do some test stitching on a practice quilt sandwich to see if your tension is better. Keep making small adjustments and testing the results until the problem is solved.

Top thread showing on back

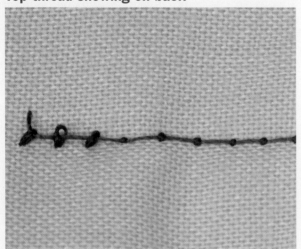

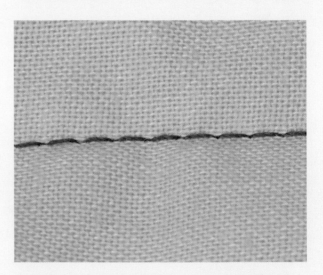

If dots of top thread are showing on the back of your quilt, it means the top tension is too loose.

To tighten the top tension on your machine move the number on the dial higher. Remember to always move the dial in tiny increments until you solve the problem.

adjusting the bobbin tension

If you are unable to solve your machine's tension problems by adjusting the top tension dial, an adjustment to the bobbin tension may be needed. Check your machine's instruction manual for suggestions on adjusting your bobbin tension. These guidelines will also assist in making adjustments.

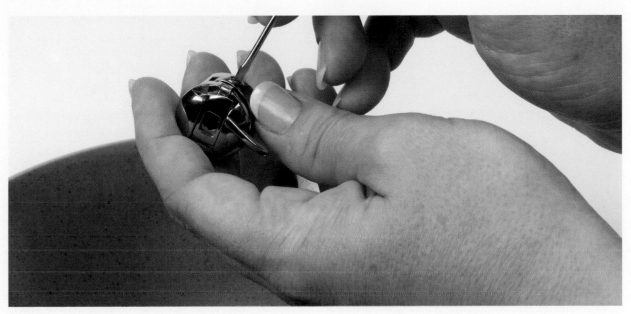

If dots of bobbin thread are visible on the quilt top, you will need to tighten the bobbin tension. If your machine has a removable bobbin casing, hold it in one hand with the screw facing you. If your machine's bobbin casing is not removable, locate the tiny screw located near the bobbin. Using a tiny screwdriver, turn the screw to the right in very small increments to tighten the bobbin tension. Sew a line of practice stitches to see if the tension has been adjusted correctly.

If dots of the top thread are showing on the back of your quilt, you will need to loosen the bobbin tension. To do this, turn the screw of the bobbin casing to the left. Always remember to turn this screw just a tiny bit at a time. It is very sensitive.

It is easy to lose the bobbin casing screw if you loosen it too much. To avoid this place a bowl under the bobbin casing while you work with the screw, or place your hands in a plastic bag when you make adjustments.

Call in a professional

If you will be using several different types of thread when you quilt, it is a good idea to buy a second bobbin case. Use it for making big adjustments to the bobbin tension. If your machine does not have a removable bobbin casing, ask a service technician or salesperson to show you how to adjust the bobbin tension correctly.

tension troubleshooting

- **Oil and clean your machine regularly.**
  Make it a habit to clean and oil your machine regularly. It will last longer and produce better machine quilting stitches. Have your machine serviced yearly by a professional.

- **Use the right needle for the right thread.**
  Experiment with different needles if you're having trouble balancing the tension. If you are in doubt about which needle to use with which thread, check with your local quilt shop. Checking the web page of the thread company for the thread you are using can also be a great source of information regarding which needle works best.

- **Replace the needle of your machine.**
  A dull needle could be the cause of your thread tension problem. Try changing to a new needle if you're having problems and know it's been awhile since you've inserted a new needle.

- **Rethread the top and bobbin threads.**
  Rethreading the top and bobbin threads can sometimes solve the problem and is usually the first thing I try when sudden tension problems occur.

tip

Disguise the problem

Using the same color and weight thread in the bobbin and on the top can eliminate, or mask, tension problems.

Small prints on the back of your quilt will help disguise your quilting stitches. This makes them a great choice for those times when your tension may be good, but not perfect.

keeping the top the top

The beauty of free-motion quilting is that you can quilt in any direction and never have to turn the quilt. This is a good habit to form right from the start. It is especially important when working on large quilts that cannot be rotated or turned as you stitch. Train yourself to not rotate your quilt. Keep in mind that when you put a small quilt in your sewing machine, the side that is farthest away from your body (and in back of the machine) is the 'top' edge, and needs to stay in this position at all times. It can be tempting to let yourself turn a small quilt in order to see your stitching better, but do not give in to this temptation, or you will find it very frustrating when working on larger pieces.

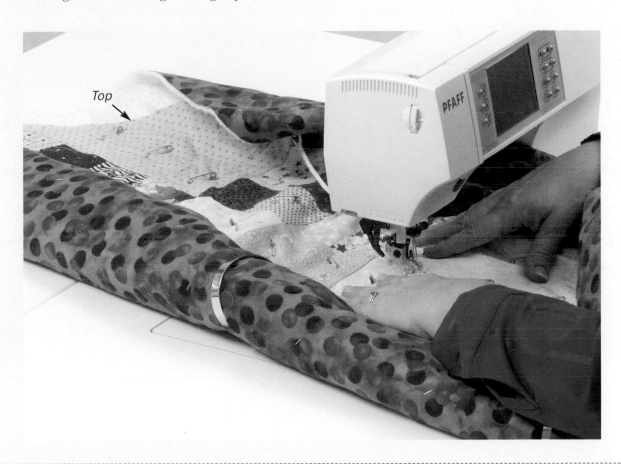

Top

techniques

You'll find several different types
of quilting techniques on the
following pages. I suggest practicing
each quilting until you are
comfortable with your results.
Before you know it you'll be ready
to quilt a family heirloom.

beginning doodling

I like to use the word "doodling" when talking about free-motion quilting. It conveys the idea of something that is easy, relaxing, and fun. There are no rules that need to be followed when you doodle and it's a great way to learn how to machine quilt. If you enjoy doodling on paper you are already on the way to becoming a great free-motion machine quilter.

"L" Loops

It's easy to become good at free-motion quilting, when you stitch shapes already familiar to you. Loops that resemble a lower-case, cursive "L" will allow you to become familiar with the motions needed for this type of stitching.

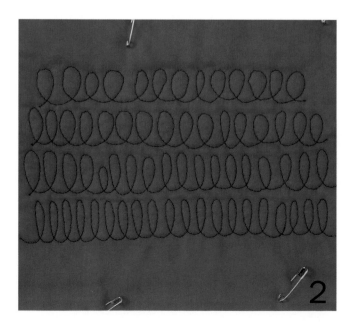

Put the free-motion foot on your sewing machine, lower the feed dogs, and place a plain practice quilt sandwich beneath the needle. Bring up the bobbin thread and secure the first stitches. Activate the needle down feature on your machine, if you have it. Begin stitching slowly, focusing on controlling your stitch length as you move the quilt sandwich under the needle. Using your hands to guide the quilt sandwich, control the speed of the needle with the amount of pressure you put on the foot pedal. Relax and stitch a few L-shaped loops. Practice coordinating the movements of your hands with the pressure of your foot on the foot pedal. This takes time and practice, but is important to master at the beginning. Use any stitch length you like as long as you strive for consistency from stitch to stitch. Always keep the top edge of your practice quilt sandwich in the same position as you stitch. Move it around freely, but do not turn it.

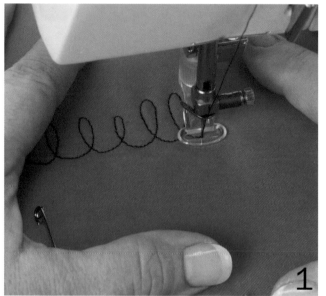

Doodle another line of L-loops, focusing again on moving the quilt sandwich and the foot pedal in rhythm. If your stitch length looks too long, slow down the movements of your hands, or press harder on the foot pedal as you stitch. If your stitches are too short, speed up your hand movements, or ease up on the foot pedal. If your L-loops are not smooth and rounded, try speeding up the movement of your hands and machine. Take your time and cover the entire quilt sandwich with L-loops. You'll be able to see an improved progression between your first L-loops and your final ones.

"C" Stitches

Lines of "C" stitches are great for developing the movements needed to quilt beautiful feather designs. Feather designs require stitching back over the same line of stitches, as you do when quilting the letter "C".

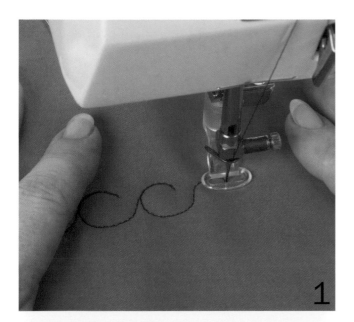

Begin by bringing up your bobbin thread and securing your beginning line of stitching. Begin to move the quilt sandwich so your stitches create the top curve of a cursive letter "C".

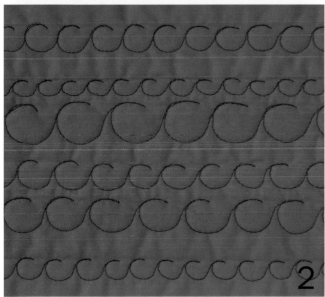

Retrace the top curve of the "C" and continue bringing your line of stitching down to create the lower curve to finish the letter. Stitch as many "C" shapes as you can on the quilt sandwich. Make some large and some small. Keep practicing. This stitch is essential when creating feather designs.

"Quilter's gloves are very helpful, but I often use a little Neutrogena® hand cream instead of the gloves. Be sure to rub it in well. Either one will help you keep a good grip on the fabric and reduce the amount of stress on your arms and shoulders."

tip

Get a grip

Keep a good grip on the fabric under the needle. This is important for eliminating the possibility of puckers on the back and front side of your work.

practice patterns

When you are comfortable with the coordination it takes to control your stitch length, cover a few practice quilt sandwiches with these patterns. Stippling resembles the curved edges of puzzle pieces. It is basically stitching without any corners or straight lines. The scale of stippling can go from tiny stitching to a very large-spaced design used to fill in background areas. Before you start practicing, check your tension and make any adjustments necessary. Refer to thread tension on pages 23-26 for more information.

Medium-Sized Stippling

Bring up the bobbin thread and secure the beginning stitches. Clip the beginning threads.

Start stitching medium-sized smooth, rounded shapes. Achieving smooth and rounded stippling will take practice. Stippling will take time and patience to master, but it is well worth the effort.

To move to another space in your quilt sandwich, continue stippling into that area, and it will appear as if it belongs in the design.

Stippling

Try stippling in different scales with the curved lines and the distance between stitching lines varying in size. Keep in mind that consistency is pleasing to the eye and continue moving your hands smoothly as you press on the foot pedal.

"Some people like to assign rules to stippling, such as not crossing over previously stitched lines. If you find you have to cross lines to get from one space to another, make a point to do it several times so it looks like part of your overall pattern."

For stippling different types of blocks/quilts

As you fill in around appliqué or patchwork, take care in planning your progression from one area to the next. This will reduce the number of times you will need to stop and start.

When you stipple quilt on a patchwork block, you can stitch in the ditches of the block to go from one area to another.

Hooks and Curves

Try playing with angles, or add hooks to your lines of curved quilting.

Loops and Stars

Experiment with stars and loops. I add the loop between the stars because it helps reposition the needle for starting the next star.

tip

If your stitches are uneven

speed up and see if your stitches become more uniform. If your stitches are too long, move your hands slower or speed up the machine. If your stitches are too little, move your hands a bit faster or slow down the machine.

"I learned small mistakes are not a big deal. I've quilted bobbles but didn't want to stop stitching and correct at that time. Later when I tried to find my mistake, I could not see it anywhere, no matter how hard I searched."

tip

Do not stitch

over or too close to the safety pins in your practice quilt sandwich or in any quilt project. If the pins lie within 3" or 4" of the needle, stop and remove them before you continue stitching.

advanced doodling

When you feel you've mastered the beginning doodling designs, it's time to take the next step to advanced doodling. As you practice, try not to get caught up in making sure every stitch looks perfect. When you look at an entire finished quilt you will not notice the small imperfections. Just relax and enjoy more doodling.

Words and Letters

Most of us use cursive writing every day. You've practiced 'l's and 'c's on pages 30-31, so now you're ready to put it all together and write your name and other family names in quilting.

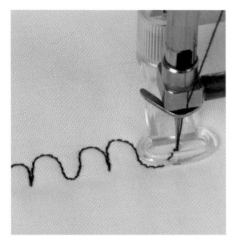 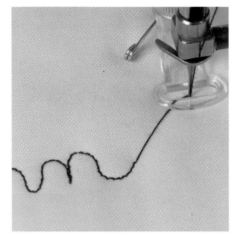 

Bring up the bobbin thread and secure your beginning stitches. Move your quilt sandwich with the same motions you would use if writing with a pen.

After stitching the first word, secure your ending stitches. Jump to where you want to begin the second word, letting the threads lie on the top and back of the quilt sandwich. Go back and clip the long threads later.

Lock the first stitches and continue quilting the next word. If there is a 't' in the word, the line crossing it needs to be made at the same time you stitch the letter. To do this, stitch outward from the vertical line on each side, making a horizontal line on either side of the vertical line and continue.

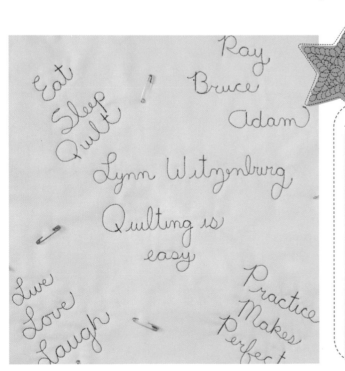

basics

Jumping is an easy way to begin a new line

of stitching without stopping to clip threads. When you are ending a line of stitching and the next line is close, take a few securing stitches, lift the presser foot, and 'jump' to the next line of stitching. Secure the beginning stitches and continue sewing. Clip the threads between the jumping points on the front and back of the quilt when you are finished quilting. Jumping will save time and thread.

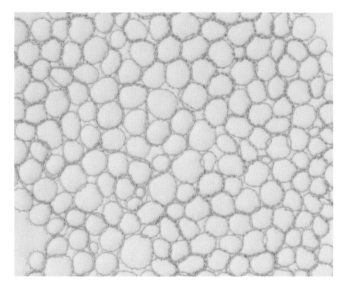

Circles

Varying sizes of circles stitched close together will resemble a cobblestone wall. This is easy once you get the hang of it. Rocks and stones are not all the same shape, so different sizes and shapes will look natural.

Snowflakes

You will be stitching over previous lines of stitching to form these flakes. Don't let that scare you. The best thing about snowflakes is no two are alike.

Flowers

1. Stitch one petal. At the base of the petal make a circle for the flower center.

2. Continue stitching petals around the center connecting to it each time.

3. When all the petals have been stitched around the center, retrace stitching lines to continue to the other side of the flower and begin making the next flower. Add leafs and veins between flowers if desired.

machine-guided stitching

Stitching in the ditch is sewing quilting stitches along the seam lines in patchwork. This is a great way to accentuate pieced designs and strengthen the seams in your quilt. Typically, I stitch all the outline or ditch stitching on my quilt first. This stabilizes the quilt and allows you to remove many basting pins. If you have done a good job basting, you can begin stitching on any area of the quilt.

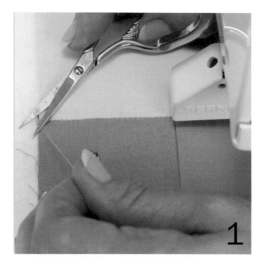

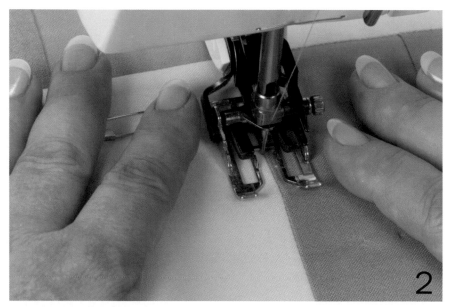

Attach the walking foot, raise the feed dogs, and place your quilt sandwich in the machine. The first seam you want to stitch should be under the needle. Bring up the bobbin thread and secure the beginning stitches. Take a few stitches and clip the threads.

Grip the fabric on either side of the needle and pull seam apart firmly. This will flatten the fabric and make the seam easy to see. Start stitching directly into, or as close to, this seam line as possible. Keep a good grip on the fabric as you stitch. Stitch to the end of the seam. Secure stitches and clip the threads. Place the quilt sandwich in position for stitching the next seam and repeat directions above for each seam you want to stitch.

tip

Stitch control

Since the machine is guiding the fabric, it will control your stitch length. Adjust it using the stitch length regulator on your machine to get the length you prefer. There are no rules, so use the stitch length that appeals to you.

free-motion stitching

Using a free-motion foot for stitching in the ditch enables you to quilt in any direction without turning your quilt. Use a free-motion foot for any ditch quilting that does not extend from one end of a quilt top to the other.

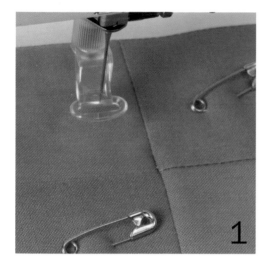

Attach the free-motion foot, lower the feed dogs, and place your patchwork quilt sandwich in the machine. The first seam you want to stitch should be under the needle. Bring the bobbin thread up and secure the first stitches. Clip the beginning threads.

Grip the fabric on either side of the needle and pull the seam apart. Stitch directly into, or as close to, the seam line as possible. As you practice, don't be concerned with hitting the ditch perfectly with every stitch. The more you practice the better your stitching will become.

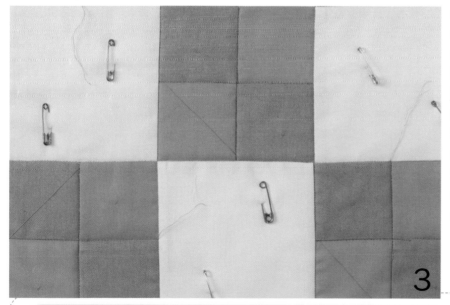

Continue stitching in the ditch of each seam. Stitch as far as possible without stopping. This may take some planning but will save time in the end. You can jump from one stopping point to the next starting point and clip the connecting threads later. Remember that you can go any direction necessary without turning the entire quilt. When you reach an area where you can't stitch any farther, secure and clip the threads.

No walking

Limit your use of the walking foot to stitching the seams that run the full width or length of your quilt. Overuse of the walking foot can become a habit and create frustration when you're stitching a large quilt that is difficult to turn. Practice stitching in the ditch with the free-motion foot as much as possible. It will speed up the process significantly.

choosing a stencil design

There are many great quilting stencils on the market and it can be intimidating choosing which ones to use on your quilts. Continuous-line designs, the ones you can quilt from beginning to end, without stopping or jumping, are the best choice for machine quilting. Visit your local quilt shops and check out their selection of stencils. If it is not immediately apparent which ones are continuous-line designs, ask for help in choosing a practice stencil. Quilting a marked design is different from the free-motion quilting you've been practicing. I mark designs on the quilt top after the basting has been done. The basting process allows me time to look at the quilt top and formulate ideas about how it should be quilted.

Marking Lines and Curves

 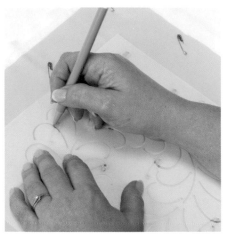 

Center the stencil design in the desired quilting area. When marking a quilting design using a stencil, it is not necessary to take out basting pins.

Mark in the lines of the stencil with a marking tool. Use a blue wash-out marker if your fabric color is light or a white or gray chalk pencil if the fabric is dark.

Be sure to mark all lines carefully. If there is a safety pin in the line of marking, mark up to it, and reach under the stencil to flip the pin to its other side and mark the area missed. Carefully check under the stencil to be sure all the marking lines are visible.

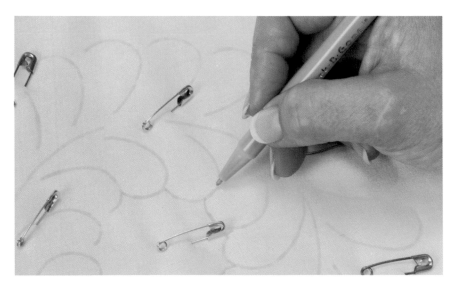

Marking Connecting Lines

After all the lines are marked, remove the stencil and connect the interrupted lines. This will help you become familiar with the stitching flow of the design. Stencils are designed with interruptions within the design lines that are there to hold the stencil together. These lines were meant to be connected when stitched.

working with quilting paper

Quilting paper gives you the advantage of not having to mark your quilt top with a marking pen or chalk pencil. It can also make it easier to create your own designs.

Marking Single and Repeat Motifs

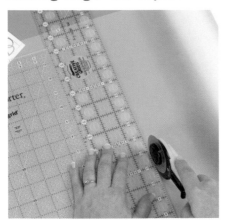

Using a rotary cutter, mat, and ruler, cut a piece of quilting paper 1" to 2" larger than the size of the quilting design.

Using the fine-line permanent marker, center and trace the design onto the quilting paper.

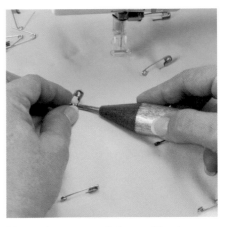

Place the area of the quilt where this design is to be stitched on a flat surface. Remove safety pins from this area only.

Center the quilting design in the area to be quilted. Replace the basting pins catching the quilting paper and all layers of the quilt sandwich. Pins may be left open for easy removal.

Quilt the design by following the markings on the paper. Keep a good grip on the quilt to ensure it is lying flat under the paper.

Repeat Motifs

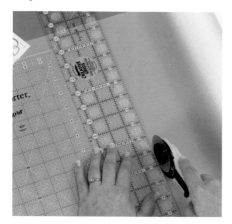

Using a rotary cutter, mat, and ruler, cut the number of pieces of quilting paper needed for the repeat motifs in your quilt. Cut these papers 1" to 2" larger than the size of the design.

Using a fine-line permanent marker, trace the design onto one piece of quilting paper for every 15 motifs needed.

Place the number of plain quilting paper pieces you need (no more than 15) in a stack. Place the marked design on top. Secure the papers together with straight pins.

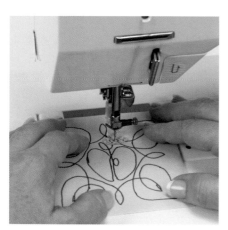

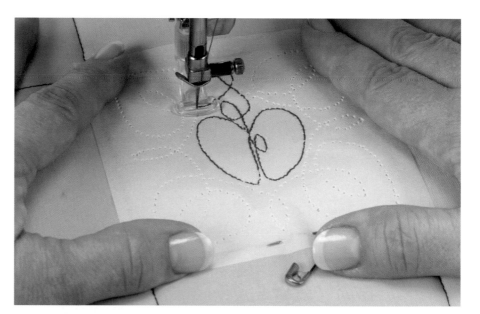

Remove the top and bobbin threads from your machine. Place the stack of quilting papers under the needle and stitch the lines of the marked design, perforating all the layers. Stitch carefully and smoothly, the holes on the unmarked papers will eventually be your quilting guide. Once you have started the perforation process, you can remove the straight pins. The stack will hold itself together.

Rethread your machine. Place the area of the quilt where the design is to be stitched on a flat surface. Remove the safety pins from this area. Peel off one of the designs from the perforated stack and center the design in the area to be quilted. Replace the safety pins, catching both the paper and the quilt sandwich as you pin. Stitch the design on top of the paper. Keep a good grip on the quilt to be sure it is lying flat under the paper.

Removing Quilting Paper

Removing quilting paper from a stitched design is simple. Sit down and tear. However, there are a few tricks to make this process faster and more thorough.

Run your fingertips under the quilt, gently pulling where the paper is attached. It will separate in several places loosening many of the pieces.

After the larger pieces of quilting paper are removed you will find smaller pieces that are caught under your stitches. Use a pair of sharp-pointed closed scissors to press on those pieces and carefully pull them out. A small pair of tweezers will also work.

"I have been asked if perforating the paper dulls my needle. In my experience, I have not noticed this to be a problem."

tip

Quilting paper

can be purchased in most quilt shops or from architectural and engineering suppliers. Quilt shops carry the Golden Threads brand which comes in three sizes and is golden in color. Architects and engineers use the same type of paper, but have other choices in size and color.

When drawing or tracing designs onto quilting paper, always use a fine-line permanent marker. Ink from other types of pens will migrate onto the thread and ultimately end up on the quilt.

Perforating more than 15 pieces of quilting paper at a time results in larger holes in the bottom sheets. This causes them to come apart more easily and makes them more difficult to use.

When I use quilting paper on very light fabrics, I make a few extra perforated designs so I won't need to use the one with the drawn design. The paper marked with black lines becomes very visible on a light-colored quilt. Even the smallest pieces left behind will show.

adapting motifs to fill spaces

Patchwork quilts often have oddly shaped areas to be quilted. Use quilting paper to play with stencil designs and create or adapt designs to fill in those areas. Adapting part of a design that will be repeated in another area of the quilt is always a great idea.

Filling Oddly Shaped Spaces

To create quilting designs for shapes that do not fall into the category of traditional squares, triangles, or rectangles, rotary cut a piece of quilting paper approximately 1" larger on all sides than the oddly shaped patch in the quilt.

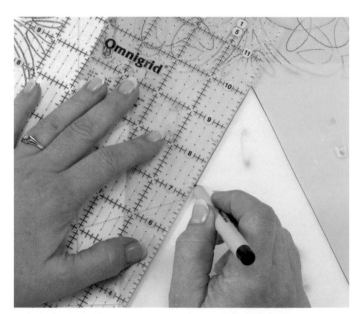

Lay the piece of quilting paper over the oddly shaped patch. Trace the patch shape onto the paper, using the fine-line permanent marker. Use a very light touch, so the paper doesn't tear causing accidental marks on the quilt top.

Lay the marked shape over various machine quilting designs until you find something you like. You can trace parts of many designs to come up with something new. Try to connect the lines so you create a continuous-line design. This process doesn't take an artistic flair; it just takes patience and experimentation. You may find that tracing several copies of the outline made from the quilt top will be necessary before you find just the right design.

background designs

Filling in a large plain background can be challenging for anyone. A great way to give your quilt a traditional hand-quilted look is to use uniform background designs.

Free-motion Marked Background Designs

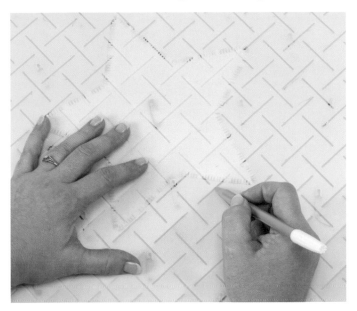

Use a blue wash-out marker or chalk pencil to mark a grid of cross-hatched lines on your fabric. Large background stencils allow you to line up the design with the edges of the area being marked. They also make matching the lines when moving the stencil easier. These stencils are available at quilt shops and craft stores

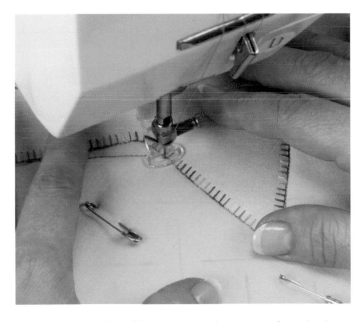

Stitching cross-hatching or any other type of marked background design is easiest when using a free-motion foot and your feed dogs dropped.

This allows you to stitch in every direction and makes it possible to stitch in the ditch over to the next starting place. You can also jump to start the next line of quilting.

When quilting paper doesn't work—use a stencil

I don't use quilting paper on large background areas, because it shifts too easily, which makes it a challenge to keep straight lines straight.

free-motion unmarked background designs

When quilting large free-motion unmarked designs in background areas, follow these suggestions.

Keep starts and stops to a minimum

- Before you begin stitching it may be helpful to do some sketching on a piece of paper to determine how to keep your design continuous. You do not need to mark background designs such as echo quilting, stippling, or other doodling types of design.

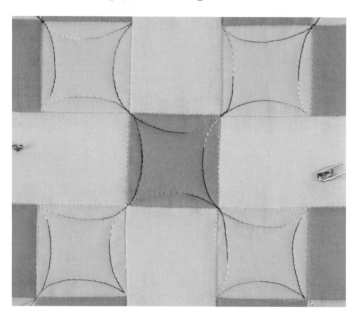

Try stitching crescents

- Use simple crescent shapes that go from corner to corner on four-patch or nine-patch quilt blocks. Crescents are completely continuous, lots of fun to stitch, and can be done on an entire quilt without stopping. They are also a great way to add curves to a quilt top that is mostly straight lines. Don't worry if the arcs aren't all exactly the same on your crescent shapes. The end result will still be spectacular.

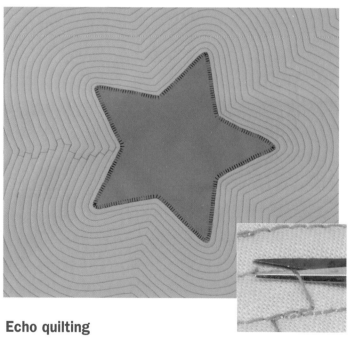

Don't stitch yourself into a corner

- Try not to get yourself trapped in an area you can't stitch out of without stitching across a previous line or stitching where you weren't planning to. If this happens, jump or stitch in the ditch to get to the next unquilted area.

Echo quilting

- Echo quilting is an effective way to accentuate a pieced or appliquéd design. It does not need to be marked. Strive for the same amount of space between quilting lines. As you complete each revolution around the design, take a few securing stitches and jump to begin the next round. Clip the threads when you have completed the block.

quilting border designs

There are a few basic things to know about making quilting designs fit in the border of a quilt. For example, when you purchase border designs, be sure that the design includes a way to turn the corner. However, if a border design you want to use does not come with a corner design, it is possible for you to create one of your own, following the techniques below.

Creating Corner Designs

Cut a square of quilting paper at least twice as big as the width of the border design you will be using. For example; if your chosen border design is 4" wide, cut a piece of quilting paper that is at least 8" to 10" square. Draw lines on the paper to replicate a 4" corner of the border on the quilt.

Using the border design you've chosen, find a part of the design that would look nice when placed at an angle in the corner of the marked 4" square. Sometimes, you'll have to play with the border design in order to find the best way to fill the corner area. Careful consideration will be needed to allow for connections between your newly created corner design and the straight portion of the border design to keep a continuous flow going.

Draw the rest of the design on both sides of the corner to complete your corner design.

making border designs fit

Once you have a corner design that works, the corner must always be used on the quilt exactly as it is drawn. Follow these steps to make sure that the border designs will fit your quilt correctly.

Cut four squares of quilting paper that are larger than the corner design. A different example is, if your border design is 5" wide, then cut the quilting paper for the four corner squares at least 10" x 10". This will give you plenty of space to draw your corner design, plus a portion of the straight part of the design on either side. Draw the corner design on one square and then stack the remaining three squares underneath it. Hold the four corner squares together with straight pins.

Estimate how many repeats of the border sections you will need by dividing the width of the roll of quilting paper into the length of each of the borders. The way I actually do this is less than technical. I take the roll of quilting paper and just "bounce" it along the border of the quilt for a quick estimation of how many strips it will take to make the design go from one corner to the other, then I typically add one or two more strips, just to be safe. Cut the number of strips of quilting paper equal to the estimated number for all 4 sides of the quilt. Trace the border design on one quilting paper strip for every 15 strips you will need to fit around your quilt's border. Stack the strips of quilting paper together in groups of 15 or fewer. Put the marked design strip on top, and hold them together with straight pins. With your machine unthreaded, stitch over the drawn lines, perforating the stacks of quilting paper. Repeat for the four corner paper squares.

Place your layered quilt sandwich on a flat surface, so that one side of the border lies perfectly flat. Remove all of the safety pins from this border. Pin the quilting paper strips into place, taking care to keep the area that is unpinned flat at all times. Pin two of the corner designs in place at the two corners of the border.

Rarely do the border designs fit a quilt border perfectly. Decide whether it is easier to make your border design longer or shorter. If you need to lengthen it, find a place in the design where it will be easiest to add small amounts of space. Cut the quilting paper strips in these places and spread the paper apart to lengthen your border design. Making multiple small adjustments is less noticeable than making one or two large adjustments.

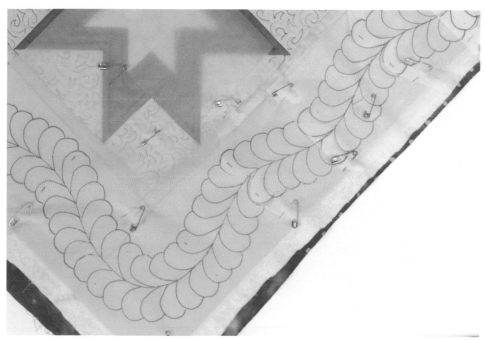

If you need to shorten the border design, find a place in the design where space can be easily removed, and cut the paper and overlap it at that point. Repeat as many times as needed to make the border design strips fit your quilt. Again, it is always easier and less noticeable to make multiple small adjustments than a few large ones. Once you are satisfied with your design adjustments, pin the strips into place, using safety pins and being careful to keep the back and batting flat.

tip

It just takes more

It will take more safety pins to pin the multiple pieces of quilting paper than the number it took to initially baste the border. You'll want to be sure that each individual piece has enough safety pins in it to keep it from shifting as you quilt.

You have a choice as to whether you want to quilt one side of the border at a time, or pin the design strips around your entire border before you begin to quilt. On very large quilts, I stitch one border at a time and leave the safety pins open because it is easier to pull them out quickly, while stitching. If I pin the border quilting paper on all 4 sides of the quilt, I close all the pins with a Kwik Klip™, because as the quilt folds in on itself, the safety pins will hook on each other and pull out. You will also get your fingers pricked too often.

stitching feathers

Feather quilting designs make the simplest pieced quilt look elegant. When I took my first machine quilting class, we were not shown how to do feathers. I just always assumed that they were very hard to stitch, and that you needed to be a very accomplished machine quilter to be able to master them. A few years later, I took a machine trapunto class. When the teacher handed out the quilting design we were to use in class, it was a feather wreath. I was frozen in my seat! She continued talking, saying that feathers were indeed continuous designs. Since I have never been a quiet and shy person, I blurted out, "Prove it!" Once she had demonstrated how to quilt feathers, I realized that not only were they continuous, but they were not nearly as difficult as I had led myself to believe. That is why I always demonstrate how to do feathers in every machine quilting class I teach. It only takes practice to master the elegant curve and flow of this beautiful design.

Round Feather Wreaths

A round feather wreath is the best feather design to begin practicing. It is repetitive in the way it is stitched. There are typically more feathers around the outside of a round wreath and fewer in the center part. You'll want to start with an outside feather.

Begin by pulling up the bobbin thread in the "cleavage" of one of the marked outside feathers and secure the first stitches.

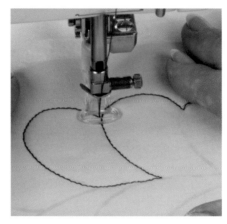

Start stitching around the first feather until you reach the vein. Stitch along the vein to the next feather. Stitch that feather, stopping at the cleavage.

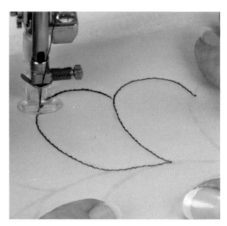

To stitch the next feather, you must stitch back over the previous line of stitches. This is the same technique used to stitch "Cs" in Beginning Doodling. Stitch back over the same line of quilting to where the next feather starts, and stitch that feather down to the vein.

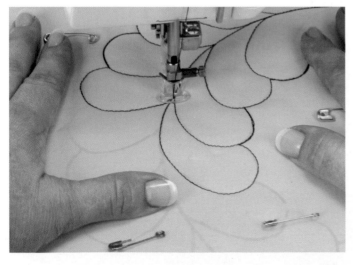

Stitch on the vein to connect what has already been stitched. Stitch back along the vein to get to the next unstitched feather, whether it is in the center or on the outside of the wreath. You'll be alternating between the feathers in the center and the ones on the outside depending on which one connects to the vein next. Continue stitching on that feather until you get to the cleavage, then stitch back over the same line along the top to get to the next unstitched feather.

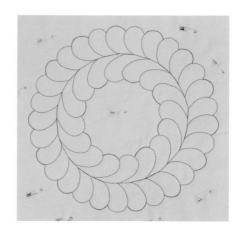 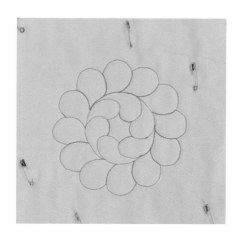

Always retrace the shortest line of quilting as you stitch each feather. Feathers will vary in width and length. For short, fat feathers backstitch along the sides of the feathers, rather than the top. It is okay to stitch over a line that has already been stitched in order to reach the next area.

Square Feather Motifs

There are many different shapes of feather designs. The ones with a square look are nice, because they usually fill a block out to the corners. They are quilted in the same manner as a round feather wreath.

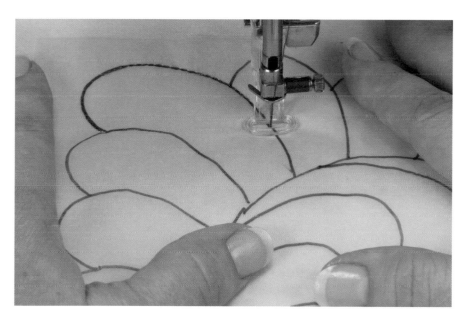

Pull up the bobbin thread in one of the large corner feathers and secure the beginning stitches. Stitch the first feather.

Continue stitching around the design in the same manner as a round feather wreath.

As you may be able to see in this photo, I backstitched along the side of two of the large corner feathers. There are no rules, so if it is a shorter distance to backstitch on the side rather than over the top, go for it.

Triangular Feather Motifs

Triangle feather designs are stitched differently than others. There is no definite progression to follow, because I can stitch the same design several times and end up doing it a different way each time. Triangle feather designs differ from one another, so you may need to use your ingenuity when tackling a new one. The one thing that stays the same is where to begin.

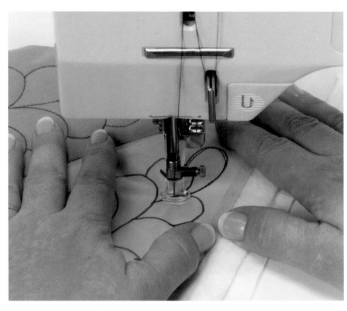

Pull up the bobbin thread on the feather that is the farthest to the right or left of the design and secure the first stitches. Complete the first feather.

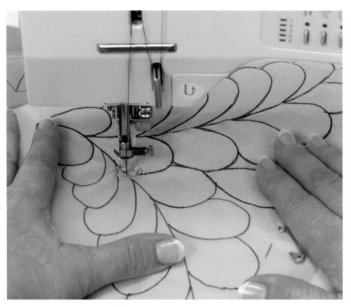

Determine the shortest route to the next feather. Depending on your design, you may need to stitch on a previously stitched line.

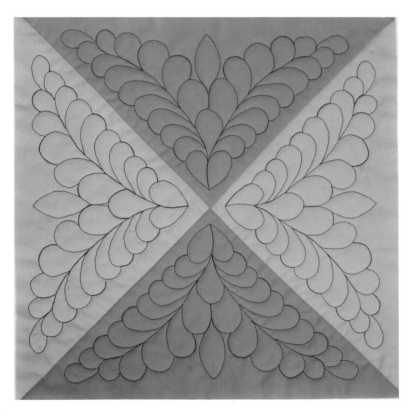

Continue stitching from one side to the other, making sure to connect the vein as you go. You'll need to be aware of where you need to stitch next. Always strive to retrace the shortest distance possible.

Freeform Feathers

Freeform feather designs can be done many different ways. They look great, even when the feathers are varied in size.

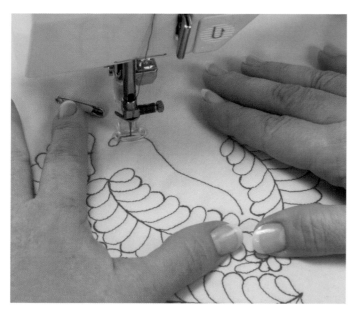

Bring up the bobbin thread and secure the beginning stitches. To begin your design, stitch the vein of the feather.

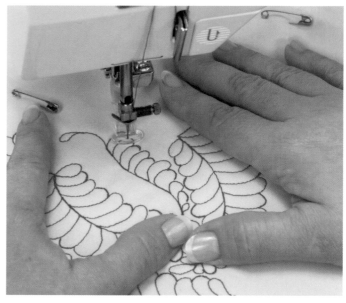

Secure and clip the ending threads. Move to the bottom of the vein and start stitching feather shapes up one side.

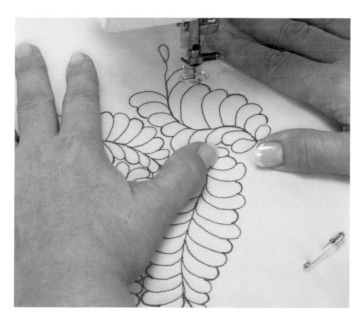

Vary the size and shape of the feathers to fit the space you are trying to fill. After the first side of feathers is done, secure and clip the threads. Go back to the beginning to stitch the other side.

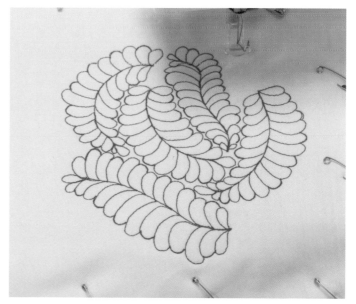

After practicing stitching each side of the vein separately, try filling in both sides at the same time. It's a little more tricky, but saves time with fewer stops and starts.

Adapting Feather Designs

Feathers are easy to manipulate. If you have an oddly shaped area on a quilt, it is easy to draw a feather design to fit it. The feathers do not have to match to be beautiful. Try quilting some feathers without marking.

Corner Feathers

Stitching the corner feathers follows the same guidelines as Creating Corner Designs on page 45. The corner designs must remain the same while any adjustments needed must be made in the straight borders.

Feathered Border Designs

Feathered border designs are an elegant way to frame a quilt. It is easy to make any adjustments needed to get a perfect fit on your quilt.

A single vein feathered border design can be stitched in a continous line.

A double vein feathered border design will need to be stitched in two passes around the quilt. Stitch one side of the feathers all the way around and then jump to the opposite side to complete the design.

"If a feather design has a double vein, stitch all of the outside or inside feathers as one unit. Stop and jump to the opposite side and stitch those as one unit. This also applies to border feather designs."

Don't be intimidated

It can be easy to get lost when you get back to the top of a feather. This is a good time to stop and see where you need to go next. Don't panic. Relax and you'll achieve a nice, smooth stitching rhythm.

If you don't hit the line when stitching a feather the first time, stay on the stitched line if you retrace it. Remember the marked line will disappear when you remove the markings, so your error will show less if you keep the two lines of stitching on top of each other.

bobbin quilting

The vast array of threads available can enhance a quilt's beauty. Unfortunately, some of the most beautiful threads are too heavy to go through the top tension bars of the sewing machine. In cases like these, bobbin quilting is the answer. Bobbin quilting is done by stitching from the back side of a quilt with the heavier, decorative thread meant for the top of the quilt placed in the bobbin, and the thread meant for the back of the quilt threaded through the top of the machine.

Water-Soluble Thread

- If your quilt does not consist of a block and border format you may need to position your quilting designs on the front side of the quilt. This can be done by stitching the design with water-soluble thread in both the top and bobbin of the sewing machine. Place your design in the desired position on the front of the quilt, pin into place, and stitch. Rethread your machine with the heavy decorative thread in the bobbin and lighter weight thread on the top. Restitch the design from the back of the quilt. Mist or wash the quilt to remove the water-soluble thread.

Stabilizing Stitching

- Stitching in the ditch of the blocks and border seams is what I refer to as 'stabilizing stitching' and is the first step to take when starting the quilting process. This creates guidelines for placement of quilting designs on the back side of the quilt.

Center quilting design on back of quilt using stitched line for placement.

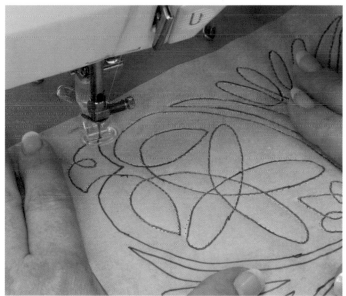

With heavy decorative thread in bobbin and regular thread in top of the sewing machine, stitch design on marked lines.

Once the design is completely stitched turn the quilt over to reveal the beautiful thread on the front of your quilt.

"Store water-soluble thread in a sealed plastic bag to protect it from moisture and humidity. If you use this type of thread in moderate-to-high humidity, problems with breakage could occur. I try to do projects using water-soluable thread only in the driest winter months."

thread and tension guidelines

Using a lighter weight synthetic thread, such as polyester, rayon, or monofilament, opposite a heavy decorative thread may be helpful in achieving better tension balance. Test your thread combination on a scrap quilt sandwich to make sure your top and bottom tension are going to be balanced in your finished quilt. Often, you will need to loosen the bobbin tension significantly in order to achieve good tension with heavier weights of thread.

 t i p

Make your mark

To mark your quilting designs directly on the fabric, use a water-soluble marking pen for light-colored fabrics or a chalk pencil for dark fabrics.

Just in case

Sewing machine technicians recommend buying an extra bobbin case to use for bobbin work. The screw on a bobbin case is very sensitive. It will not stand up to repeated adjustments if you plan to switch back and forth from heavy to regular threads.

making trapunto easy

Trapunto is a fancy word for stuffed work. It sounds intimidating, but once you see how it's done, you'll be amazed at how easy it is to add this elegant dimension to your quilts. Trapunto should be done on a completed quilt top. All the piecing or appliqué must be complete and the quilt top ready to be quilted. Select which areas of your quilting designs you want to stuff and where you want to place the designs.

Getting Started

Cut pieces of quilt batting at least 1" to 2" larger than the size of the quilting designs you wish to stuff.

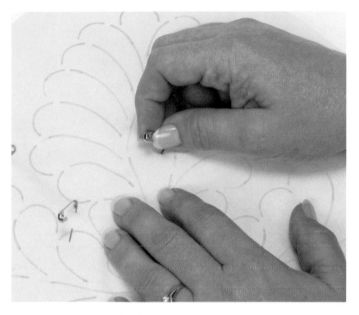

Mark the quilting designs on your quilt top, using a water-soluble marker for light fabrics or a chalk pencil for dark fabrics. Place two pieces of batting underneath a Trapunto area on the quilt top and pin in place. I use open safety pins because they are easier to remove than straight pins.

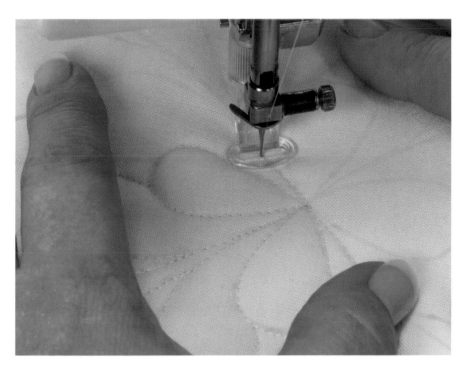

Thread your machine with water-soluble thread on top and a light-weight cotton thread in the bobbin. Use a thread color to match the batting. Remember to loosen the top tension. Stitch the Trapunto area of the quilting design. Be careful to keep the two layers of batting flat. Some battings slide more easily under the needle than others. If it feels a bit "sticky," you may have to use a little more muscle—but don't give up.

You'll need to cut away the batting in the areas not intended to be stuffed. It can be challenging to do this without cutting the quilt top. Finding the best scissors for this task is tricky too. If the scissors are too pointed, it is easy to snip into the fabric of your quilt top. If they are not pointed enough, it can be hard to get into the tiny corners. Experiment to find the pair of scissors that works best for you. Appliqué scissors work best for me. I use the non-billed side of the scissors in the fabric and carefully snip away at the batting being careful not to clip the fabric.

Layer and pin-baste the practice quilt, as you would normally, placing a full layer of batting between the backing and quilt top.

"For Trapunto areas, I like to use batting that is 80-percent cotton and 20-percent polyester. The polyester gives the stuffed area a bit of loft, and will hold it better than cotton."

*tip

Snippets

If you accidentally made a small snip into the fabric when you were trimming the batting from the Trapunto areas, take a couple of extra quilting stitches on top of the cut when doing the final quilting. If you are planning to quilt with a decorative thread that contrasts with the background fabric, be sure to first use a lightweight, matching cotton thread to take the extra stitches needed to secure the snipped area.

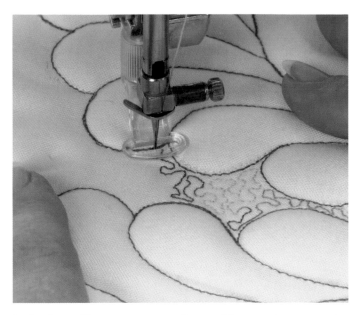

Quilt the quilt as you normally would, except you must stitch the Trapunto areas again on top of the water-soluble thread.

Trapunto looks best when close, tight filler quilting, such as stippling, is placed around it.

t i p

It's breakable

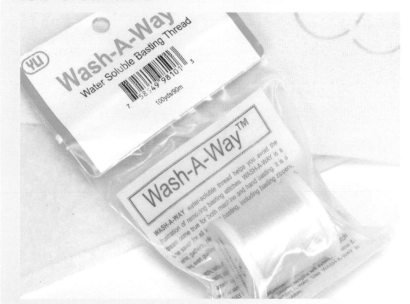

Water-soluble thread plays a major role in this technique. It tends to break easily in the sewing machine so try to avoid using it in times of high humidity. Loosen the top tension on your machine as much as you can, while still getting stitches that are secure.

Paper jams

I have found that using quilting paper for Trapunto presents a challenge, because the higher loft of the double batting layers causes the paper to rip easily. If you have an adjustment for the height of the pressure foot on your sewing machine, quilting paper may still be an option for you.

Quick fix

If you make a large cut, you may need to take a scrap of matching fabric, apply fusible web to the right side of it, and fuse a piece just large enough to cover the cut on the back side of the quilt top.

quilting a full-size quilt

The thought of quilting a large quilt often creates a feeling of panic for many quilters. Don't be intimidated— you can do it. Getting a quilt ready for machine quilting is one of the most important steps in the entire quilting process. Your quilt will be moved, turned, and stuffed into the small area to the right of the needle as you stitch, so carefully basting the layers together is the key to preventing puckers in your finished work.

backing and batting sizes

The backing and batting must always be larger than the quilt top. How much larger depends on the size of your project. To calculate the size you need for the backing and batting in a project, I recommend adding at least 2" to 3" to each side measurement of the quilt top for smaller quilts. As the size of your quilt top increases, so should the amount added to the backing and batting. Add at least 6" to 8" inches for a double-size top and 8" to 10" inches for a king- or queen-size quilt top. Always double check the batting package to be sure that the size you are buying will be large enough for your project.

Making Seamed Backings

For quilt tops that are 38" to 40"-wide or less, you can use a single length of 45"-wide fabric, and simply cut a piece that allows 2" to 3" extra around each edge of the quilt top. For example: if a quilt top measures 40" x 52", cut a length of 45"-wide fabric, 54" to 56" long. For quilts that are wider than 40", you will need to make a backing with a seam in it. Here are two ways you can prepare a seamed backing for a quilt project.

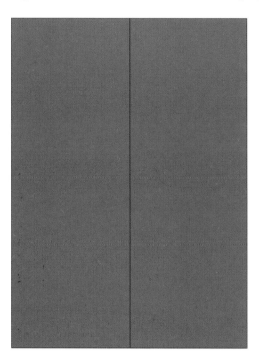

- To make a backing for a medium-size quilt, you can often achieve this task with one seam. To do this, measure the width and length of your quilt and add at least 4" to each side measurement to determine the necessary size for the backing. Cut two lengths of fabric to this length (or width, depending on the size of your project), and rotary cut the selvage edge from one side of each length. Sew the two trimmed edges together. Press this seam allowance open to reduce bulk. For example: If your quilt top measures 56" x 68", cut 2 lengths of 45"-wide fabric, 60" each. Trim selvages and stitch together along trimmed edges. Backing will be approximately 84" x 60".

- To make a backing for a large quilt, you will often need 3 lengths of fabric. To do this, measure the dimensions of your quilt top and add 6" to 8" to each measurement. Cut three lengths of fabric to this measurement, trim the selvages and sew the three panels together, placing one length at the center, with the other two lengths on either side. Press these seam allowances open. For example: if your quilt top is 82" x 100", cut 3 lengths of 45"-wide fabric, 90" each, trim selvages and stitch together. Your backing will measure approximately 126" x 90".

Loose threads

If your backing is a light color, use a lint roller on both the backing and the batting before you smooth the batting out. This will remove any stray threads, which can really show through after the quilting is finished. If your quilt top has light-colored areas, you'll also need to remove stray threads from the wrong side of it.

There are fabrics on the market today that are specifically meant for quilt backings. These vary from 90" to 108" in width, which means that you would not have to have seams in your backing at all.

Take care when using a directional print for a pieced back. Be sure the print on all lengths of the fabric is going in the same direction.

You may choose to use a generous amount of spray starch when you press the backing fabric before assembling the layers of a quilt sandwich. This will help keep it smooth and free of wrinkles and help eliminate the possiblity of puckers in your finished quilt.

Basting surfaces

Whether you use the floor or tables, basting the backing, batting, and quilt top together into a quilt sandwich is just plain physical work—there is just no other way to describe it. Basting on top of tables rather than on the floor is much easier on the back. Two or even three 8'-long tables pushed together, depending on the size of the quilt top, is how I baste my quilts. It's best to use as many tables as needed so that the least possible amount of the quilt top hangs over the edges. As a general guideline, I try to never allow more than 6" to 8" of a quilt top to hang on each side of the basting surface.

You can usually find large tables to use for basting a quilt sandwich together in your local quilt shop's classroom, libraries, and churches. Just call and ask if they will allow you to use a few of their large tables for this purpose. Most places are very accommodating when they know what you wish to do. Just remember the table surface may have some scratches on it when you are finished.

Basting with Safety Pins

 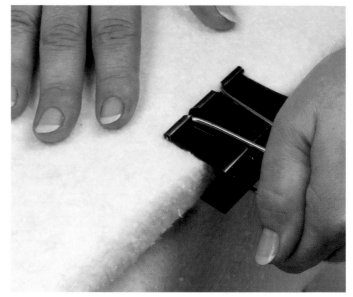

Place the backing wrong side up on a flat basting surface. If you work on a floor, you will need to use masking tape. If you use a table with a lip around the edge, binder clips are very handy to keep the edges in place. **It is extremely important that the backing be taut, but not stretched.** If the backing is stretched before you baste the layers together, it will go back to its original size afterward, and your quilt will have built-in puckers! Use masking tape or binder clips every 6" to 8" around the edges of the backing.

Center the batting on top of the backing, and smooth it out. If you used binder clips to hold the backing in place, and you find that there are lumps in the batting that do not smooth out easily, gently flatten and smooth out the batting right up to the clip. Then, while holding the batting and backing in place with one hand, remove the clip and replace it again, catching both the backing and the batting together. If you used masking tape to secure the backing, you can just add a few more pieces of tape to hold the batting in place on the backing, as necessary. Most of the time, it will not be necessary to attach the batting to the basting surface at all.

Center and smooth the quilt top over the batting, making sure that there is ample batting and backing showing around each corner and edge of the quilt top. Smooth from the center outward, taking your time to ensure that every square inch is flat and smooth.

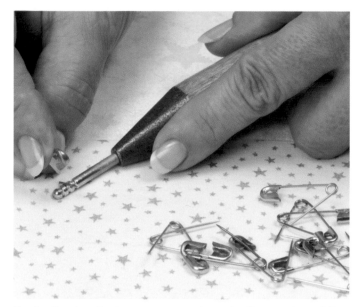

Begin the basting process as close to the center of the quilt as you can reach. The most efficient way I have found to baste a quilt is with a Kwik Klip™ basting tool. The tool allows your quilt to stay as flat as possible when inserting and closing the safety pins. Refer to page 17 for instructions on using the Kwik Klip™.

If you are not using a Kwik Klip™ basting tool, you'll need to insert all of the pins into the quilt sandwich and leave them open until you are finished; then go back and close them all. The reason for this is that when you close a pin with your finger, you must raise it quite high to get your finger under it. This will raise the backing as well and can compromise the hold of the binder clips or masking tape.

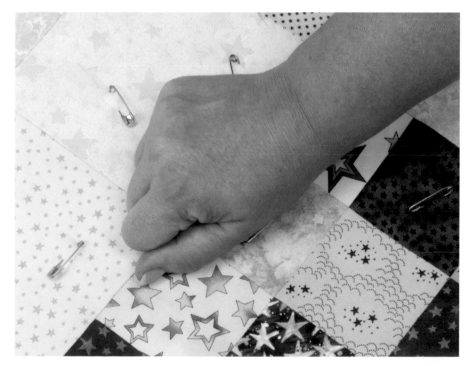

Continue adding safety pins approximately 3" to 4" apart in a random pattern across the top of the quilt sandwich, smoothing the top after each pin is placed. The pins should be no more than a "closed fist away" from each other. This means that if you can place your closed fist in any area without feeling a pin, you need to add one or two more safety pins.

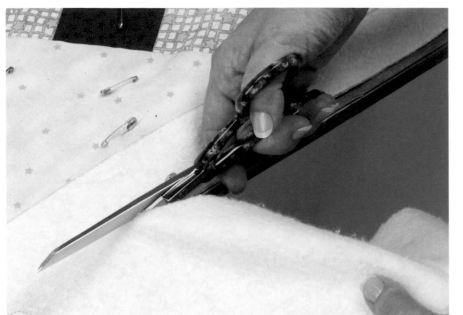

After your quilt is completely basted, trim the extra backing and batting to 1-1/2" to 2" from the quilt top, which will be a manageable amount during the quilting process.

tip

Big quilt, no problem

If your quilt top is larger than the table(s) you are working on, you will need to pin the part that lies on top of the table surface first. Then remove the binder clips and slide the quilt over so that you can pin each edge, one at a time. Be careful that all the layers lie absolutely flat before you add the last pins. Slide it on the table again, to baste each edge. I pin all the way to the edges of my quilts, so that I can avoid having the backing fold under and get stitched to itself. If your quilt is large enough that you can't reach the center, you can insert safety pins as far as you can reach and leave the center unpinned until you finish. To baste the center, remove the binder clips and/or masking tape from the backing and pull the entire quilt toward you until you can reach the unbasted area at the center; just be sure that all of the layers are flat and smooth before you place the final pins.

There are good reasons to avoid thread basting a quilt sandwich together. One is that basting stitches on the bottom of a quilt tend to get caught in the throat plate of a sewing machine. Another is that basting stitches can often get caught in your quilting stitches, making it is necessary to cut them many times to remove them completely. Safety pins are a much better option, because it is easy to take them out individually as you come to them, while the other areas of your quilt remain secure.

Using poly batt

If you are using polyester batting, you'll need to increase the number of safety pins you use to baste the layers of a quilt together. Because of the slickness of this manmade fiber, it doesn't cling to the backing and quilt top like cotton.

managing a large quilt

It is important to have your machine in a cabinet if possible when you tackle any quilt larger than a wall hanging. The bed of your sewing machine should be flush with the surrounding surface. Your quilt should have complete support with no edge of it falling over the sides.

Rolling from the sides toward the center

It is important to have family or friends around to lend a hand when rolling a twin or larger size quilt. The more hands you have helping, the tighter each roll can be which decreases the bulk of the quilt at your sewing machine.

Start with a plan of where you will begin stitching. If you want to stitch in the ditch along the sashing strips from one end of the quilt to the other, you will need to roll the side edges of the quilt parallel to that ditch. The basic rule is roll the quilt so the area to be stitched is left flat.

Lay the basted quilt sandwich flat on the floor or large table surface. Roll the edge of one side of the quilt toward the center of the area you want to quilt. Keep the roll as tight as you can, and stop rolling 6" to 8" from the area to be quilted. Slide quilter's clips onto the roll, placing them approximately 14" to 16" apart. These clips will hold the roll until you are ready to release it.

Roll the opposite side of the quilt toward the center. Stop 6" to 8" from the area to be quilted. As before, slide the quilter's clips over the roll 14" to 16" apart.

*tip

Focus

It is important to be sure all ends of the quilt are supported on the table surface. When you are stitching, your focus needs to be on the area around the needle. This makes it difficult to be aware of what the rest of the quilt is doing. It is important to fold the quilt rolls back on themselves if necessary, and keep all of it on top of the table surface. Some of my worst quilting bobbles have occurred when a part of the quilt accidentally dropped over the edge of the cabinet surface and caught, just as I am trying to move the quilt while stitching.

Positioning a Large Quilt in your Sewing Machine

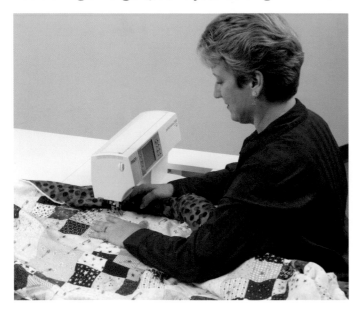

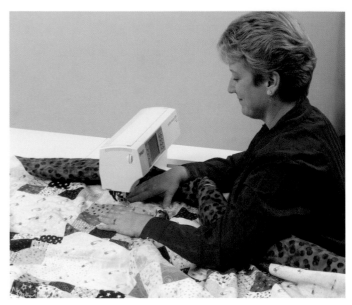

Place one rolled side of the quilt into the throat of the sewing machine with the flat part underneath the needle and the opposite roll to the left of the needle. There will be quite a bit of extra rolled quilt to manage. The priority is to be sure the area to be stitched is flat under the needle, while the rest of the quilt is supported on the cabinet and tables and out of the way of your hands. Do whatever is necessary to quilt the area under the needle and let the rest go where it may. Many times I have part of the quilt over my shoulder or rolled up on my chest.

Quilt as much as possible in that vertical 12" to 16" unrolled area of the quilt.

As you quilt the full length of the 12" to 16" flat area of the quilt, unroll the part of the quilt in the throat of the machine a few inches at a time. Quilt the revealed length of the next area.

Continue quilting and unrolling the same roll until you can quilt the remaining areas without having the quilt rolled.

Remove the quilter's clips, turn the entire quilt around, and put the opposite roll into the throat of the machine. Proceed in the same manner, quilting and unrolling, as before.

You will need to re-roll the quilt several times in the quilting process. The following suggestions will assist you in managing your quilt.

- Roll the long sides toward the center to stitch in the ditch of vertical rows.

- Roll the short sides toward the center to stitch in the ditch of horizontal rows.

- Re-roll the long sides toward the center to stitch in the ditch within blocks.

- Re-roll the long sides toward the center to do detail stitching within blocks.

Sliders

If a quilter's clip gets in the way of your hand or arm as you prepare to quilt, slide it up or down the roll until it is out of the way.

If a quilt is set diagonally, it is best to roll it diagonally to do the initial quilting.

quilting for display

The order in which you stitch a quilt is important, especially if you are going to hang the quilt on a wall or display it in a quilt show. If the quilt is for a bed or is going to be carried around and loved by a child, the quilting order is much less critical. Following the guidelines in this chapter, your quilts will hang with the least amount of waviness possible, assuming you are starting with a relatively flat quilt top. Because there are so many different types of quilt tops and infinite ways to quilt them, this chapter will focus on a traditional quilt pattern set in a traditional arrangement, and quilted in a traditional manner, as a basic example of this process.

Stabilizing Stitching or Ditch Quilting

The best way to begin quilting is to do what I call stabilizing stitching, or ditch quilting. These are the broad strokes of the quilting process, where you can outline and stabilize the sashing strips and borders. This is one of the only times where using the walking foot is the best choice, because you will be stitching from one end of the quilt to the other. Remember, as long as you have basted the quilt correctly, you can begin quilting anywhere.

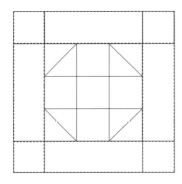

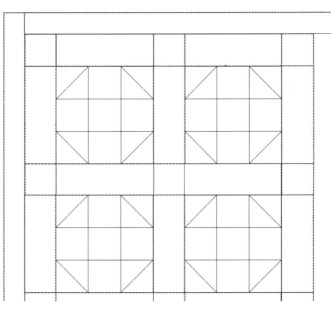

- First, stitch in the ditch on both sides of the rows of sashing strips in both directions. If your quilt is large, you may need to roll it once for the vertical and once again for the horizontal rows to achieve this task.

- Next stitch in the ditch around the border. Because I'm going to stitch a decorative design over the top of all the outer borders, I'm not going to stitch in the ditch between each one. It isn't necessary to stitch in every ditch, especially if additional quilting will go over that seam. Next, stitch in the ditch around patchwork in the blocks.

tip

Hiding in the ditch

Ditch quilting should show as little as possible in a finished quilt. To reduce the visibility of the thread for this type of quilting use a very lightweight cotton (size 60) in a matching color, if possible. If you find that there are two or more shades that are very close to the fabric color you are matching, the darkest shade will always hide in the ditch better. If stitching in the ditch will take you over many different colors of fabric, you can choose a clear or smoke-colored monofilament thread.

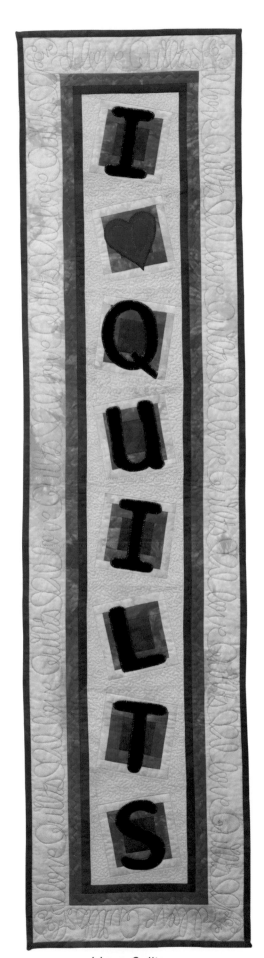

I Love Quilts

Outlining Piecing and/or Appliqué

Use a free-motion foot to do ditch stitching around piecing within the quilt blocks or around appliqué shapes.

- Drop the feed dogs on your machine and attach the free-motion foot, so you can stitch in any direction without turning the quilt. Because you can go in any direction, the churn dash block can be completely outlined without having to stop.

- Don't let the walking foot become a crutch because it is perceived to be an easier way to stitch in the ditch. Although this is true when stitching long, straight seams, it can really slow you down when it comes to stitching in the areas where using a walking foot makes it necessary to turn the quilt top.

- If your quilt has appliqué motifs, it is best to stitch around each of the appliquéd pieces within each motif. This will greatly accentuate the appliquéd elements in your quilt. Because there are generally many different colors overlapping in appliqué, using monofilament thread is always a great choice for this type of stitching. However, I love the look and feel of cotton, and I typically use a lightweight cotton thread and take the time to change the color of thread in the machine to match the appliqué piece I am outlining. Most of the time, I can get many pieces of the same color outlined in a section of the quilt before needing to switch thread colors.

- When outline stitching hand appliqué, I like to take a stitch or two on top of the appliqué in areas I know have a skimpy seam allowance. For example, the bottom 'V' of a deep inner point like the 'V' at the top of a heart, or the tip of a sharp point can be strengthened by one or two tiny, well placed outline stitches.

Adding Quilting Motifs in Open Areas of Patchwork

This is my favorite part—adding all the marked decorative quilting designs in the open spaces of the outlined areas in a patchwork quilt. If your quilt is large, you will need to re-roll it to get back into the center areas to stitch the decorative motifs you want to quilt in each block and sashing strips.

Quilting the Border

Once the decorative areas within the quilt are complete, it is time to quilt the border. Often, at this point, I can see just a little wave in the border of my quilt. This is caused by the drawing up of the center area, due to the quilting that has already been done. Just be aware that this will be an area to pay close attention to when you quilt the border. You'll need to keep a good grip on the fabric, to be sure it is flat while you're quilting it so the result will be flat after it is quilted.

Dense Quilting

The densest stitching needs to be left until the very last. This includes stippling or any other small free-motion fillers or small, dense marked designs. This type of stitching distorts a quilt top more than any other kind of quilting; leaving it until last reduces the amount of distortion, especially when quilting the borders.

One very important factor to ensure that your quilt will lie flat is to keep the density of the quilting consistent throughout the quilt. For example, if you have stitched an area with very dense stippling along with wide sashing strips that have no quilting at all, the result will be a wavy quilt. If you keep the quilting simple throughout an entire quilt, you may be able to get by with no quilting in the sashing strips. I've seen many quilts hanging in shows with very little or no quilting in the sashing strips or borders, which almost always results in a wavy quilt.

Dashes of Color

Blocking your Quilt

A process known as blocking is one more way to ensure that you will have a nice, flat quilt. Depending on the size of your quilt, you will need a large, flat area such as a floor or multiple tables to lay it out flat. The quilt itself will need to be damp, either from misting it well with water from a spray bottle, or washing it in a machine. If you wash it, you may want to dry it just until it is damp and then lay it out. Each corner of the quilt will need to be attached to the surface it is lying on. On a carpeted floor, it works well to stick straight pins through the quilt and into the carpet. The main idea is to be sure that the quilt is square by using quilters' acrylic rulers to square it and attach it to the flat surface until it is completely dry.

projects

Now you are on your way to beautiful machine quilted quilts. Here are some fun projects for you to make with the quilting design choices ready to go.

72

hot and cold running stars quilt

Finished Quilt Size: 62½" x 72½", Block Size: 10"

This quilt is a fun and easy project for quilters from beginners to advanced. The combination of warm and cool colors make this a real eye catcher!

fabric requirements

(Based on 42"-wide fabric)

15 (or more) warm-color fat quarters in reds, yellows, and oranges

15 (or more) cool-color fat quarters in blues, greens, purples, and blacks

1⅜ yards black fabric for border

1 yard green fabric for vine

½ yard fabric or scraps from stars for binding

3¾ yards backing fabric

Paper-backed fusible web

A piece of batting at least 6" - 8" larger than the quilt top (I used Mountain Mist® Completely Cotton.)

Note: Keep all scraps for stars in border.

Cutting Instructions
From each warm- and cool-color fat quarter:
• Cut 4 – 5½" squares.
• Cut 4 – 4½" squares.

Note: Border strips will be cut in Adding the Border. Binding strips will be cut in Finishing and green fabric for vine will be cut in Adding the Border Vine.

Assembling the Blocks
Note: Press all seams open when assembling the blocks.

1. Sew the 5½" warm-color squares together in pairs and then sew the pairs together to make 15 – 10½" four-patch blocks. Repeat with the 5½" cool-color squares.

Make 15   *Make 15*

2. Sew the 4½" warm- and cool-color squares together in the same manner to make 15 – 8½" warm-color four-patch blocks and 15 – 8½" cool-color four-patch blocks.

Make 15   *Make 15*

3. Trace 30 large star shapes from page 76 onto the paper side of the fusible web. Cut out the stars, leaving a scant ¼" around the outside of drawn line. Make a "window" out of each fusible web star by cutting out the center, leaving at least a ¼" to ½" of web inside the drawn line.

4. Following the manufacturer's directions, fuse the star shapes onto the wrong side of the 8-½" four-patch blocks. Carefully position each fusible web star the same distance below the top edge of the block and align the top star point and the lower indent with the vertical seam. Cut out each star on the drawn line. Peel the paper from the fusible web.

Wrong Side

5. Fuse the cool-color stars onto the right side of the 10½" warm-color four-patch blocks, taking care to line up the seams of the star with the 4 seams of the block. Repeat, fusing the warm-color stars onto the 10½" cool-color blocks.

 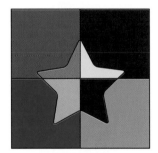

Make 15   *Make 15*

6. Finish each block by stitching around each star with a buttonhole or zigzag stitch. If desired, cut away the center of the block behind the star shape to reduce bulk when stitching is complete.

Make 15   *Make 15*

Assembling the Quilt Center

1. Lay out the blocks on a flat surface in 6 horizontal rows of 5 blocks each, alternating warm and cool blocks. Sew the horizontal rows together. Press the seams in the same direction within a row and alternate that direction from row to row.

2. Sew the rows together, pressing the seams in the same direction. Press the completed quilt center.

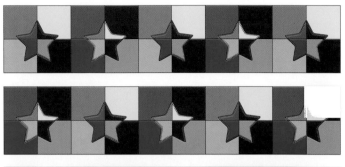

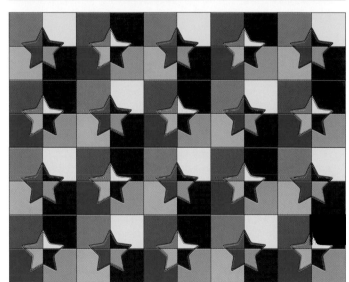

Adding the Border

Note: The following border measurements are based on the assembled quilt center measuring 50½" x 60½". If your quilt center measures differently, adjust your border sizes.

From black fabric:

• Cut 7 – 6½" strips the width of the fabric.

1. Join the 7 – 6½"-wide strips to make one long strip, using diagonal seams. Press the seam allowances open.

2. Cut 2 – 60½" side border strips and sew to the quilt center.

3. Cut 2 – 62½" top and bottom border strips and sew to the quilt center.

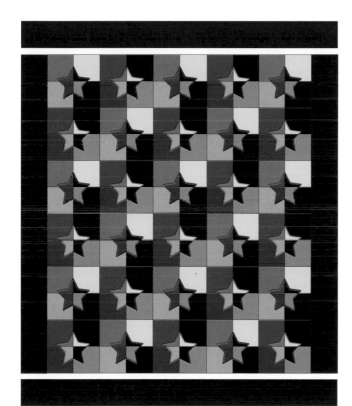

Adding the Border Vine

1. Cut ⅝"-wide bias strips from green fabric. Use diagonal seams to sew the strips together to make one long strip. Press the seams open. Fold one-third of the strip in toward the center with wrong sides together, pressing as you go down the length of the strip. Press the opposite third of the strip into the center. If desired, thread baste the seam allowances in place. Check to be sure you have at least 280" of ¼"-wide (finished) bias for the vine.

2. Lay out the quilt top on a flat surface. Arrange curving vines around the border as you please, leaving the vine at least 1" in from raw edge and border seam. Without overlapping them, place the raw ends of the strips close together. Pin the strips in place and stitch them to the border, using the same stitch you used on the Star blocks. You may need to use a shorter stitch width.

3. Trace the smaller star shapes onto the paper side of fusible web until you have 75–80 stars in a variety of sizes. Cut out the shapes from the fusible web, leaving a scant ¼" around the outside edge of each shape. Following manufacturer's directions, fuse the star shapes to the wrong side of various warm- and cool-colored scraps. Cut out each star shape on the drawn line. Repeat this process to make 130–135 leaf shapes from various green fabrics. Remove the paper from the back of the shapes and arrange them as desired. When you are pleased with the arrangement, fuse them in place. Be sure to cover the raw vine ends with stars or leaves. Stitch around each shape with a zigzag or buttonhole stitch.

Quilting

Refer to diagram on page 78 for my quilting suggestion. You may want to challenge yourself and try something completely different!

Finishing
From black fabric:

• Cut 7 – 2½" x 42" binding strips or cut enough 2½"-wide strips from fabric scraps to make 285" of binding.

1. Sew binding to the edges of the quilt.

2. Trim the extra batting and backing, leaving ¼" to ⅜" to fill the binding. Turn the binding over the edge to the back and hand- or machine-stitch in place.

3. Add a hanging sleeve and label to the back of the quilt, if desired.

Large star

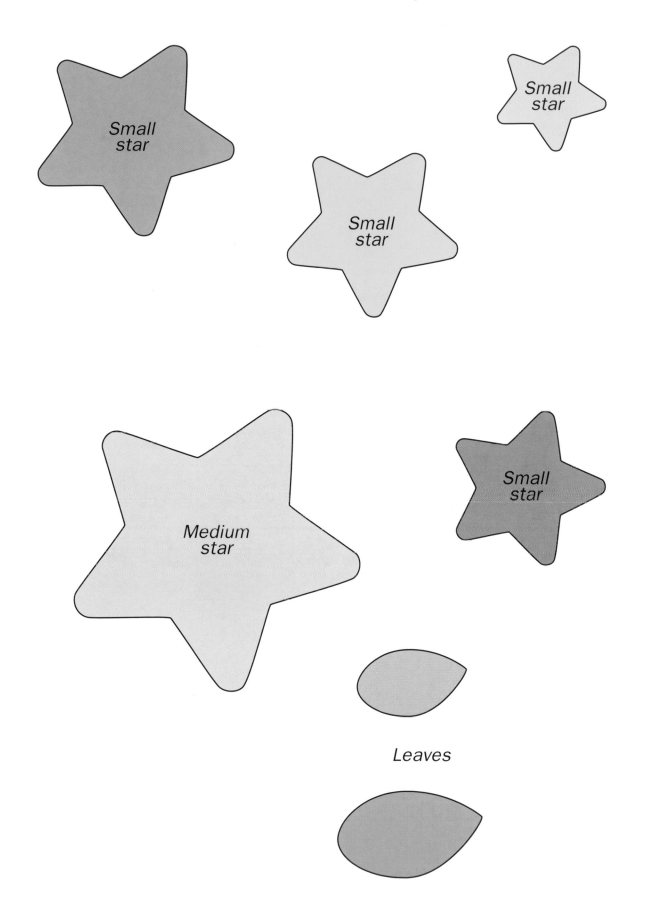

Small
star

Small
star

Small
star

Small
star

Medium
star

Leaves

Hot and Cold Running Stars Quilting Suggestion

Hot and Cold Running Stars Quilt

dancing stars quilt

Finished Quilt Size: 39¼" x 48½", Block Size: 5½"

This quilt is a fun and simple project that reflects my love for stars. Have fun making this quilt. I know your family and friends will love it as much as mine.

fabric requirements

(Based on 42"-wide fabric)

1¾ yards cream fabric for background

1½ yards dark green fabric for sashing, stems, leaves, and binding

⅓ yard pink/orange batik fabric for large stars

7 to 10 assorted batik fat quarters for border stars

1½ yards backing fabric

Paper-backed fusible web

A piece of batting at least 6" - 8" larger than the quilt top (I used Mountain Mist® Blue Ribbon Batting.)

Cutting Instructions

From cream fabric:

- Cut 3 – 6" x 42" strips.
  From strips cut:
  18 – 6" squares.
- Cut 3 – 10½" squares. Cut squares diagonally in both directions for setting triangles.
- Cut 2 – 6½" squares. Cut squares in half diagonally for corner triangles.

From dark green fabric:

- Cut 8 – 1½" x 42" strips.
  From strips cut:
  18 – 1½" x 6" sashing strips.
  29 – 1½" x 7" sashing strips.
  1 – 1½" x 8" sashing strip.
- Cut 5 – 2½" x 42" binding strips.

Note: Border strips will be cut in Adding the Border.

Assembling the Blocks

1. Trace 12 large star shapes onto the paper side of fusible web. Cut out the stars, leaving a scant ¼" around the outside of each one. Make a "window" out of each fusible web star by cutting out the center of each, leaving a ¼" to ½" frame inside the marked line.

2. Following the manufacturer's directions, fuse the large star shapes onto the wrong side of the pink/orange batik fabric. Cut out stars on the drawn line. Peel the paper from fusible web and fuse the star shapes onto 12 of the 6" squares, varying the orientation of the stars on the blocks.

Make 12

3. Stitch around each star with a buttonhole or zigzag stitch. If desired, cut away the center of the square behind the star shape to reduce bulk when the stitching is complete.

Note: Variegated polyester thread was used for the buttonhole stitch around the stars on the Dancing Stars Quilt.

Adding the Sashing

This pre-sashing method is my preferred way to make the sashing process a little easier. Instead of adding long strips of sashing to multiple blocks, the blocks have the sashing attached before the rows are sewn together.

1. Sew a 1½" x 6" sashing strip to the one edge of each of the 6 plain blocks and the 12 star blocks.

Make 6   *Make 12*

2. Sew a 1½" x 7" sashing strip to the right edge of the 6 plain and the 12 star blocks.

Make 6   *Make 12*

3. Sew a 1½" x 7" sashing strip to the left edge of 6 of the star blocks.

Make 6

4. Sew a 1½" x 8" sashing strip to the bottom edge of 1 star block.

Sashing the Setting Triangles

1. Sew a 1½" x 7" sashing strip to the left edge of 2 setting triangles.

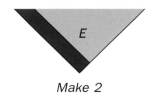

Make 2

2. Sew a 1½" x 7" sashing strip to the right edge of 3 setting triangles.

Make 3

Assembling the Quilt Center

1. Lay out the blocks according to the diagram on page 83.

2. Stitch the blocks and setting triangles together in diagonal rows. Stitch the rows together and press.

Stencil Pattern: Use this beautiful feather design for the Trapunto technique in the plain blocks.

*Enlarge Pattern
200%*

Assembling the Quilt Center

Adding the Border

Note: The following border measurements are based on the assembled quilt center measuring 30¼" x 39½". If your quilt center measures differently, adjust your border sizes.

From cream fabric:
- Cut 2 – 5" x 39½" side border strips.
- Cut 2 – 5" x 39¼" top and bottom border strips.

1. Sew the 39½" side border strips to the quilt center.

2. Sew the 39¼" top and bottom border strips to the quilt center.

Adding the Border Stems, Stars, and Leaves

1. Cut enough ⅝"-wide bias strips from dark green fabric to total at least 100". Use diagonal seams to sew the strips together to make one long strip. Press the seams open. Fold in one-third of the strip toward the center with wrong sides together, pressing as you go down the length of the strip. Press the opposite third of the strip into the center. If desired, thread baste the seam

allowances in place. Check to be sure you have at least 100" of ¼"-wide (finished) bias for the stem.

2. Trace the small star shapes onto the paper side of fusible web until you have 65 to 70 stars in a variety of sizes. Trace 60 to 65 leaf shapes onto fusible web. Cut out the shapes from the fusible web, leaving a scant ¼" around the outside of each shape.

3. Following manufacturer's directions, fuse the star shapes onto the wrong side of batik fat quarters and remaining fabric from large stars. Fuse the leaf shapes to the dark green fabric. Cut out each shape from the fabric on drawn line.

4. Lay the quilt top on a flat surface. Position the stem around the border, snaking it in and out of the setting triangles. Carefully pin the stem in place, overlapping ½" at the ends. Fold back each side where the two ends meet and pin in place. Sew the stem to quilt top using a zigzag or buttonhole stitch.

Note: Position the stem 2" away from the sashing outer points and 4" from the setting-triangle inner points.

5. Remove paper from the back of the stars and leaves and place them as desired along the stem. Use a star point or leaf to cover the stem where the two ends meet. Once you have the stars and leaves arranged, fuse them in place and stitch around each one with a zigzag or buttonhole stitch.

Quilting

I used echo quilting in the star blocks and around the border appliqué. A Trapunto feather wreath in the plain blocks is surrounded by tiny stippling.

Finishing

1. Sew binding to the edges of the quilt.

2. Trim the extra batting and backing, leaving ¼" to ⅜" beyond the quilt top to fill the binding. Turn the binding over the edge to the back and hand- or machine-stitch in place.

3. Add a hanging sleeve and label to the back of the quilt, if desired.

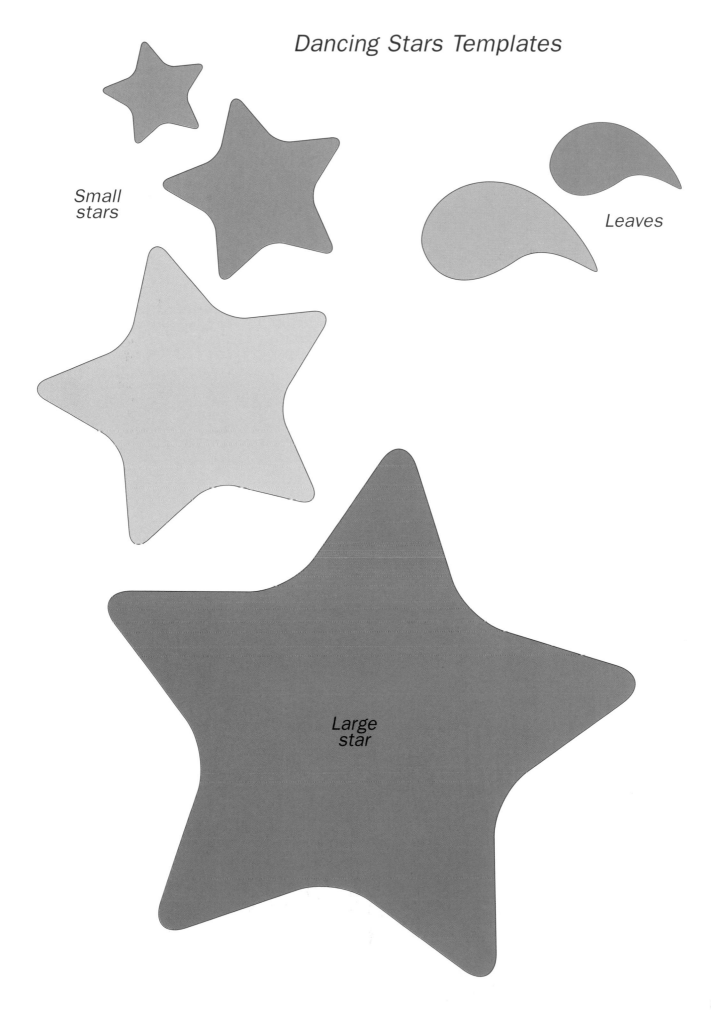

Dancing Stars Templates

Small stars

Leaves

Large star

Dancing Stars Quilting Suggestion

Dancing Stars Quilt

blazing star wallhanging

Finished Wallhanging Size: 24" x 24"

Lone Stars and Broken Star patterns have always been at the top of my list of favorites. It's a great way to play with color and contrast. Challenge yourself to try different color combinations when making this wonderful little wallhanging.

fabric requirements

(Based on 42"-wide fabric)

Note: Fat quarters do not work well for this project, because you'll need a minimum of 24"-long strips.

⅛ yard fabric #1 for star center

⅛ yard fabric #2

¼ yard fabric #3

¼ yard fabric #4

¼ yard fabric #5

¼ yard fabric #6

¼ yard fabric #7

⅛ yard fabric #8

⅛ yard fabric #9 for star tips

½ yard blue/lavender fabric for background

1 yard backing fabric

¼ yard dark blue fabric for binding

A piece of batting at least 6" - 8" larger than the wallhanging (I used Mountain Mist® Cream Rose.)

Acrylic ruler with 45-degree angle marking

Cutting Instructions

From fabrics #1-#9, cut the following number of 1½" x 42" strips:

• Fabric #1 – 1 strip.

• Fabric #2 – 2 strips.

• Fabric #3 – 3 strips.

• Fabric #4 – 4 strips.

• Fabric #5 – 5 strips.

• Fabric #6 – 4 strips.

• Fabric #7 – 3 strips.

• Fabric #8 – 2 strips.

• Fabric #9 – 1 strip.

From blue/lavendar fabric:

• Cut 4 – 8" corner squares.

• Cut 1 – 11⅞" square. Cut square diagonally in both directions to make 4 setting triangles.

From dark blue fabric:

• Cut 3 – 2½" x 42" binding strips.

Piecing the Blazing Star

1. Sew strip sets together in the following order:

    Strip Set A: #1, #2, #3, #4, #5.
    Press seam allowances toward fabric #5.

    Strip Set B: #2, #3, #4, #5, #6.
    Press seam allowances toward fabric #2.

    Strip Set C: #3, #4, #5, #6, #7.
    Press the seam allowances toward fabric #7.

    Strip Set D: #4, #5, #6, #7, #8.
    Press seam allowances toward fabric #4.

    Strip set E: #5, #6, #7, #8, #9.
    Press seam allowances toward fabric #9.

2. Align the 45-degree line of the ruler with a long edge of Strip Set A and diagonally cut 8 – 1½"-wide segments. Repeat to cut 8 segments from each set.

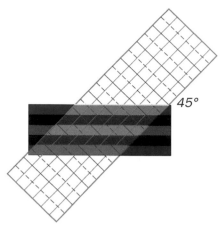

3. Pin together a segment from Strip Set A and B. To correctly align segments, use a long basting stitch to sew the two segments together. Open up the segments and check the alignment of the diamonds. If they are not correct, take out some of the basting stitches, realign, and baste again. When the alignment is correct, use a normal stitch length to sew atop the basting stitches. Continue adding one segment from each strip set in alphabetical order to complete one star point. Repeat to make 8 star points.

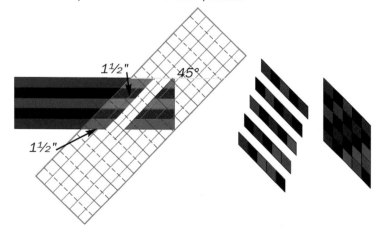

4. Sew the star points together in pairs, aligning the diamonds of Fabric #1 through #5 to make 4 pairs. Sew first with a basting stitch, realign if necessary, then finish with a normal stitch length.

5. Join the pairs to make 2 sets of 4 star points. Use the basting stitch and then a normal stitch length once the diamonds are aligned correctly.

6. Join the 2 sets of 4 star points to complete the star, stitching down the center. Be very careful about the alignment of these seams, especially the center diamonds, as mistakes will be most evident here.

Stitching the Y Seams of the Corner Squares and Setting Triangles

1. With a pencil or chalk pencil, place a dot on the wrong side of an 8" corner square at the point where the two ¼" seams would intersect at the corner. Place another dot at the point of each setting triangle where the ¼" seam allowances meet.

2. With right sides together, carefully pin one edge of an 8" corner square to one edge of an outside star point. Be sure the dot is positioned on the seam of two star points over two Fabric #5

pieces. Machine baste from the dot to the outer edge of the square. When you are sure the square is positioned correctly, sew again with a normal stitch length

3. Pin the adjacent edge of the corner square to the remaining edge of the 'Y' opening, and sew from the dot to the outer edge of the square. Repeat to set in the next corner square and then a setting triangle between the squares.

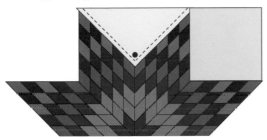

4. Continue adding corner squares and setting triangles as you work around the Y seams between the star points.

5. When all of the corner squares and setting triangles are sewn, press the completed quilt top and trim it to largest square possible. The squares and triangles are slightly larger than the star points, which allows some room for error. There will be some background fabric visible outside the tips of the star points.

Quilting

I stitched in the ditches within and around the star using Sulky® Sliver iridescent metallic thread. Various feather designs were used in the setting squares and triangles. Refer to Stitching Feathers on page 48 for tips on adding feather designs to your projects.

Finishing

1. Sew binding to the edges of the quilt.

2. Trim the extra batting and backing, leaving ¼" to ⅜" beyond the quilt top to fill the binding. Turn the binding over the edge to the back and hand- or machine-stitch in place.

3. Add a hanging sleeve and label to the back of the quilt, if desired.

Blazing Star Quilting Suggestion

Blazing Star Wallhanging

dashes of color quilt

Finished Quilt Size: 52½" x 64", Block Size: 9"

This quilt is made in jazzy, eye-catching colors, but would also look great in muted tones.

fabric requirements

(Based on 42"-wide fabric)

Note: The beautiful hand-dyed fabric in this quilt was supplied by Starr Design Fabrics from the Starr Fire fabric packs (See Resources, page 144 for information).

⅞ yard cream fabric for blocks

12 bright fat quarters for blocks

1½ yards dark blue fabric for sashing and binding

½ yard each of five bright fabrics for borders

3¼ yards fabric for backing

A piece of batting at least 6" - 8" larger than the quilt top (I used 2 layers of batting – 1 layer Mountain Mist® 95% cotton 5% wool and 1 layer Mountain Mist® 95% cotton, 5% silk.)

Cutting Instructions

From cream fabric:
- Cut 4 – 3½" x 42" strips.
  From strips cut:
  48 – 3½" squares.

- Cut 3 – 3⅞" x 42" strips.
  From strips cut:
  24 – 3⅞" squares. Cut squares diagonally to make 48 triangles.

From each of the 12 bright fat quarters:
- Cut 1 – 3½" square.

- Cut 2 – 3⅞" squares. Cut squares diagonally to make 4 triangles.

- Cut 2 – 3" squares for sashing corner squares. You will use 20.

From dark blue fabric:
- Cut 8 – 3" x 42" strips.
  From strips cut:
  31 – 3" x 9½" sashing strips.

- Cut 6 – 2½" x 42" binding strips.

Note: Border strips will be cut in Adding the Borders.

Assembling the Blocks

1. Sew 1 cream triangle to 1 bright triangle. Make 4 for 1 block.

2. Lay out a Churn Dash block according to the diagram and stitch together in rows. Press. Join rows to make 1 block. Press.

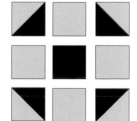 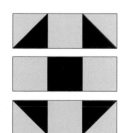 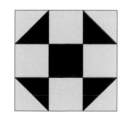

3. Repeat Steps 1 and 2 to make 12 Churn Dash blocks.

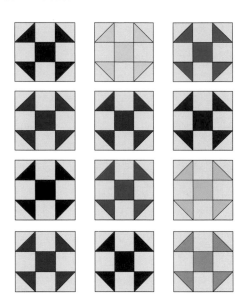

Assembling the Quilt Center

1. Lay out the Churn Dash blocks, the sashing strips, and the sashing corner squares.

2. Stitch the quilt together in rows of sashing strip/block/sashing strip and corner square/sashing strip/corner square. Sew rows together to complete quilt center.

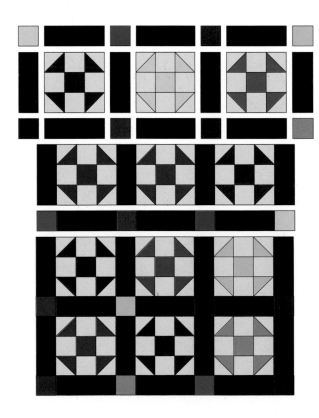

Adding the Borders

Note: The following measurements are based on the assembled quilt center measuring 37½" x 49". If your quilt center measures differently adjust your border sizes.

First Border (Light Green): Cut 5 – 2" strips the width of the fabric. Join 3 strips to make one long strip and cut 2 – 49" lengths from the strip. Cut the remaining 2 strips to 40½" lengths. Sew the 49" strips to the sides of the quilt center. Sew the 40½" strips to the top and bottom of the quilt center.

Second Border (Gold): Cut 5 – 2" strips the width of the fabric. Join 3 strips to make one long strip, and cut 2 – 52" lengths from the strip. Cut the remaining 2 strips to 43½" lengths. If your fabric is narrower than 43½", join the 2 strips with the scrap from the first two lengths before cutting. Sew the 52" strips to the green side borders. Sew the 43½" strips to the green top and bottom borders.

Third Border (Orange): Cut 6 – 2" strips the width of the fabric. Join together 2 sets of 3 strips each to make two long strips. Cut one strip into 2 – 55" lengths. Cut the remaining strips into 2 – 46½" lengths. Sew the 55" strips to the gold side borders. Sew the 46½" strips to the gold top and bottom borders.

Fourth Border (Dark Pink): Cut 6 – 2" strips the width of the fabric. Join together 2 sets of 3 strips each to make two long strips. Cut 1 strip into 2 – 58" lengths. Cut the remaining strips into 2 – 49½" lengths. Sew the 58" strips to the orange side borders. Sew the 49½" strips to the orange top and bottom borders.

Fifth Border (Magenta): Cut 6 – 2" strips the width of the fabric. Join together 2 sets of 3 strips each to make two long strips. Cut 1 strip into 2 – 61" lengths. Cut the remaining strips into 2 – 52½" lengths. Sew the 61" strips to the dark pink side borders. Sew the 52½" strips to the dark pink top and bottom borders.

Quilting

The quilting designs used in the Dashes of Color quilt were designed by Sherrie Silber. Refer to pages 134-137.

Finishing

1. Sew binding to the edges of the quilt.

2. Trim the extra batting and backing, leaving ¼" to ⅜" beyond the quilt top to fill the binding. Turn the binding over the edge to the back and hand- or machine-stitch in place.

3. Add a hanging sleeve and label to the backing of the quilt, if desired.

Dashes of Color Quilting Suggestion
(See pages 134-137 for stencil designs)

Dashes of Color Quilt

falling leaves quilt

Finished Quilt Size: 42½" x 54½"

This quilt is a simple pieced top accentuated by the quilting. The backing fabric you choose will dictate your quilting design.

fabric requirements

(Based on 42"-wide fabric)

20 to 30 dark batik fat quarters

⅜ yard dark blue batik for binding

1¾ yards of batik for backing fabric. Choose a fabric that can be used as a quilting design.

A piece of batting at least 4" - 6" larger than the quilt top (I used Mountain Mist® Blue Ribbon cotton batting.)

Cutting Instructions

From each fat quarter:

• Cut 3 or 4 – 2½" x 22" strips.
  From each strip cut:
  2 – 2½" x 11" strips.

Note: If you have more than 20 fat quarters cut 2 or 3 – 2½" x 22" strips from each.

From dark blue batik fabric:

• Cut 5 – 2½" x 42" binding strips.

Assembly Instructions

1. Sew strips together in sets of 3. Press seams one direction. Cut strip sets in 2½"-wide segments.

2. Join segments to make long rows of 21 squares each. Scatter the fabrics to create a scrappy look. Continue until you have 27 rows of 21 squares each.

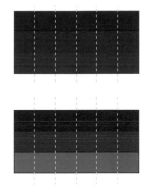

Make 27

3. Lay out rows on a flat surface and arrange until the fabrics are as mixed as possible. Sew rows together.

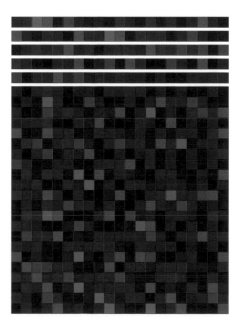

Quilting

This quilt was quilted from the back using the design in the backing fabric as my quilting pattern. The leaves were outlined with 30-weight Sulky® cotton thread. I filled in with loops between the leaves with Superior Threads Rainbows™ Polyester. Be sure the thread you use on the pieced side contrasts in color to the fabrics for the most visibility.

Finishing

1. Sew binding to the edges of the quilt.

2. Trim the extra batting and backing, leaving ¼" to ⅜" beyond the quilt top to fill the binding. Turn the binding over the edge to the back and hand- or machine-stitch in place.

3. Add a hanging sleeve and label to the backing of the quilt, if desired.

Stitching using the backing fabric as your design

A backing fabric with a definite pattern such as flowers or leaves, can become a quilting design. When stitching around the motifs on the backing fabric you are creating a coordinating motif on the quilt front. The *Falling Leaves* quilt, below was quilted from the back using 30-weight thread in the bobbin which contrasted in color with the quilt top's fabric. It was quilted from the back, and the leaf pattern on the backing fabric made a beautiful quilting design on the front.

Falling Leaves Quilting Suggestion

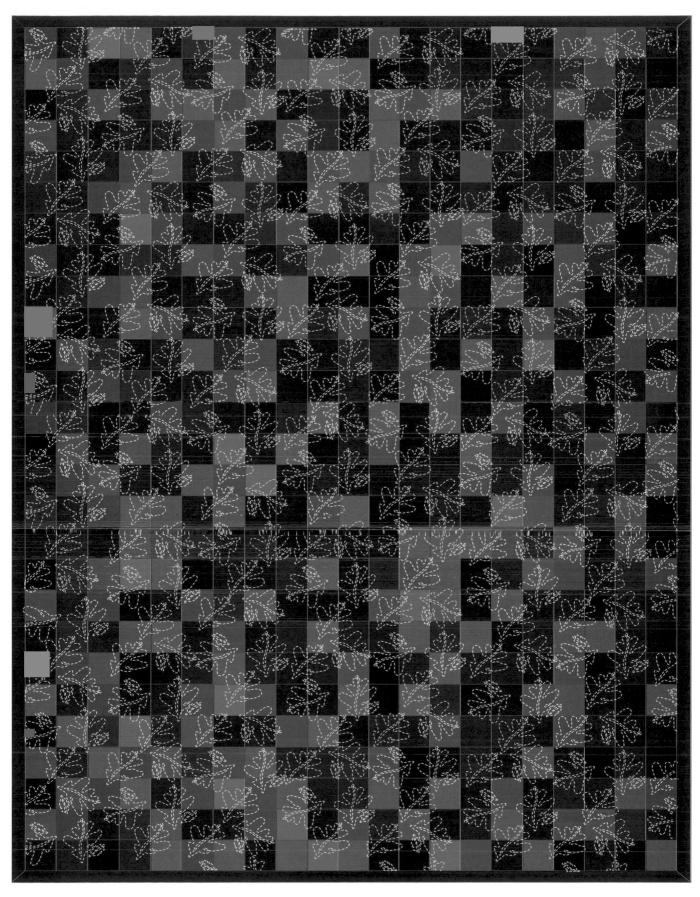

Falling Leaves Quilt

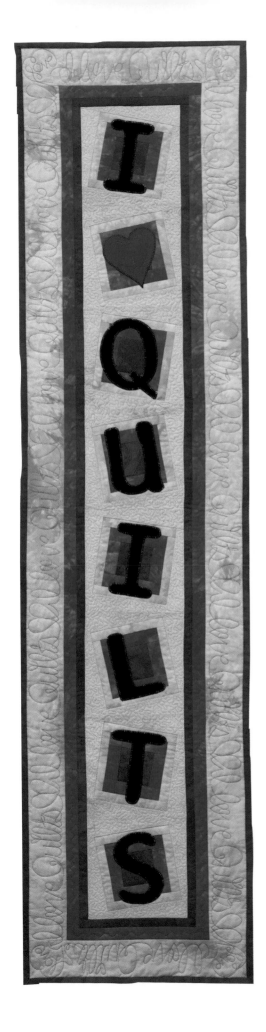

Color Option

I love quilts! wallhanging

Finished Quilt Size: 55½" x 13½", Block Size: 6"

What a great way to tell everyone how you feel about quilting! I had fun making this wallhanging and I hope you will too.

fabric requirements

(Based on 42"-wide fabric)

Note: The beautiful hand-dyed fabric in this quilt was supplied by Starr Design Fabrics from the Starr Fire fabric packs (See Resources, page 144 for information).

¾ yard dark pink fabric for blocks, border, and binding

¼ yard orange fabric for blocks and border

½ yard yellow fabric for blocks and border

Fat quarter in dark fabric for letters

½ yard cream fabric for background
(or a fat quarter)

1 yard backing fabric

A piece of batting at least 2" - 4" larger than the wallhanging (I used Mountain Mist® Completely Cotton.)

Paper-backed fusible web

Note: A 6½" square ruler is very helpful for this project

Cutting Instructions

From dark pink fabric:

• Cut 8 – 2½" squares.

From orange fabric:

• Cut 16 – 1¼" x 2½" rectangles.

• Cut 16 – 1¼" x 4" rectangles.

From yellow fabric:

• Cut 16 – 1" x 4" rectangles.

• Cut 16 – 1" x 5" rectangles.

From cream fabric:

• Cut 6 – 2" x 42" strips.
From strips cut:
    16 – 2" x 5" rectangles.
    16 – 2" x 8" rectangles.

From dark pink fabric:

• Cut 4 – 2½" x 42" binding strips.

Note: Border strips will be cut in Adding the Border.

Piecing the Blocks

1. Sew 1¼" x 2½" orange rectangles to the side edges of each 2½" dark pink square. Press.

2. Sew 1¼" x 4" orange rectangles to the top and bottom edges of the 2½" dark pink squares. Press.

3. Sew 1" x 4" yellow rectangles to the side edges of the unit. Press.

4. Sew 1" x 5" yellow rectangles to the top and bottom edges of the unit. Press.

5. Sew 2" x 5" cream rectangles to the side edges of the unit. Press.

6. Sew the 2" x 8" cream rectangles to the top and bottom edges of the unit. Press.

Adding the Letters

1. Trace the letters and heart shape on pages 107-108 onto the paper side of fusible web. Cut out the shapes, leaving a scant ¼" around the outside of each one. Following the manufacturer's instructions, fuse the letters to the wrong side of the dark fabric.

Fuse the heart shape to the wrong side of the dark pink fabric. Cut out each shape on the drawn line.

2. Peel the paper from fusible web and center the letters and heart shape on the blocks. Following the manufacturer's instructions, fuse the shapes in place on the blocks. Finish each block by stitching around each letter or heart shape with a buttonhole or zigzag stitch.

3. Using the 6½" ruler, cut the blocks to 6½" square. Angle the ruler on the blocks so the first block tilts to the right, the second to the left and so on for each block.

4. Stitch the blocks together in a long vertical row, checking to be sure they are in the right order.

Adding the Borders

Note: The following measurements are based on the assembled center blocks measuring 6½" x 48½".

Adjust your border sizes if your quilt top measures differently.

Dark Pink Border: Cut 3 – 1" strips the width of the fabric and join the three strips to make one long strip. Cut strip into 2 – 48½" lengths and 2 – 7½" lengths. Sew the 48½" strips to the sides of the wallhanging, and sew the 7½" strips to the top and bottom of the wallhanging.

Orange Border: Cut 3 – 1¼" strips the width of the fabric. Join the three strips to make one long strip. Cut strip into 2 – 49½" lengths and 2 – 9" strips. Sew the 49½" strips to the sides of the wallhanging. Sew the 9" strips to the top and bottom of the wallhanging.

Yellow Border: Cut 4 – 2¾" strips the width of the fabric. Join the four strips to make one long strip. Cut the strip into 2 – 51" lengths and 2 – 13½" lengths. Sew the 51" strips to the sides of the wallhanging. Sew the 13½" strips to the top and bottom of the wallhanging.

Quilting

The quilting designs used in the I love quilts! wallhanging were designed by Sherrie Silber. Refer to page 138.

I stitched in the ditch around the letters and in the blocks, and used cobblestones or simple stippling in the background behind the letters.

Finishing

1. Sew binding to the edges of the wallhanging.

2. Trim the extra batting and backing, leaving ¼" to ⅜" beyond the wallhanging top to fill binding. Turn the binding over the edge to the back and hand- or machine-stitch in place.

3. Add a hanging sleeve and label to the backing of the wallhanging, if desired.

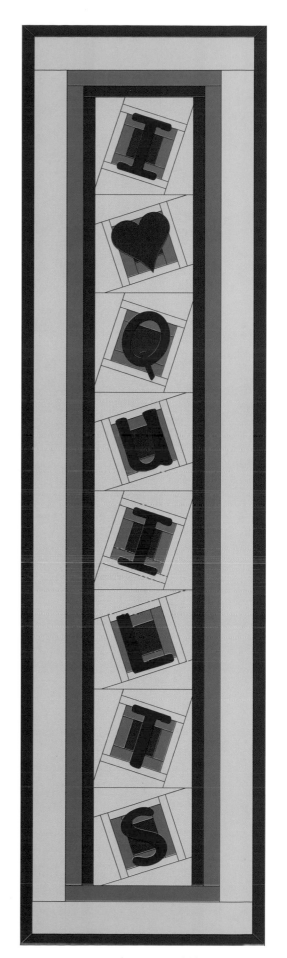

I Love Quilts Quilting Suggestion
(See page 138 for stencil designs)

I Love Quilts Wallhanging

northern lights quilt

Finished Quilt Size 21½" x 21½", Block Size: 3"

This little quilt made its first appearance in the May/June 2004 issue of *Love of Quilting*. I have made several quilts with Tri-Recs™ stars and have always loved the way they look.

fabric requirements

(Based on 42"-wide fabric)

¾ yard multi-colored fabric for blocks, setting pieces, and border

¼ yard yellow fabric for blocks and flange

⅜ yard black print fabric for sashing, inner border, and binding

¾ yard backing fabric

A piece of batting at least 2" - 4" larger than the quilt top (I used Mountain Mist® Completely Cotton.)

Tri-Recs™ Ruler set

Cutting Instructions:

Note: When using the Tri-Recs™ Rulers, fold the strips in half the long way to cut two triangles at a time or stack 2 strips wrong sides together. The bottom "recs" triangle will be the reverse of the top one.

From multi-colored fabric:

- Cut 2 – 1¼" x 42" strips.
  From the strips cut:
  72 "recs" triangles, reversing half of them.
  9 – 1¼" squares for the star centers.

- Fussy-cut 4 – 3½" setting squares for best color placement.

- Fussy-cut 4 – 3⅞" squares for best color placement. Cut these squares in half diagonally to make 8 setting triangles.

- Fussy-cut 2 – 3⅛" squares for best color placement. Cut these squares in half diagonally to make 4 corner triangles.

From yellow fabric:

- Cut 3 – 1¼" x 42" strips.
  From the strips cut:
  36 "tri" triangles.
  36 – 1¼" squares.

From black print fabric:

- Cut 2 – 1" x 42" strips.
  From the strips cut:
  18 – 1" x 2¾" side sashing strips.
  18 – 1" x 3¾" top and bottom sashing strips.

- Cut 3 – 2¼" x 42" binding strips.

Note: Fabric for borders will be cut in Adding the Borders.

Assembling the Blocks

1. Referring to the Tri-Recs™ directions, sew 2 multi-colored "recs" triangles to each yellow "tri" triangle to make 36 triangle-within-a-square units.

Make 36

2. Sew together 4 triangle-within-a-square units, 4 – 1¼" yellow squares, and 1 – 1¼" multi-colored square as shown. Repeat to make 9 star blocks.

Make 9

3. Sew the 1" x 2¾" black side sashing strips to opposite edges of the star blocks. Sew the 1" x 3¾" black top and bottom sashing strips to the remaining edges of the blocks. Press each block carefully and trim to 3½" with the star centered.

Assembling the Quilt Center

1. Lay out the block, setting squares, setting triangles, and corner triangles in diagonal rows as shown.

2. Sew the blocks and setting pieces together into rows, pressing the seam allowances away from the star blocks. Sew the rows together and press the completed quilt center.

Adding the Borders

Note: The following measurements are based on the assembled quilt center measuring 13¼" x 13¼". Adjust your border sizes if your quilt top measures differently.

From the yellow fabric:

• Cut 2 – ¾" x 42" strips.
  From the strips cut:
  4 – ¾" x 13¼" flange strips.

From black print fabric:

• Cut 2 – 1¼" x 42" strips.
  From the strips cut:
  2 – 1¼" x 13¼" side inner border strips.
  2 – 1¼" x 14¾" top and bottom inner border strips.

From multi-colored fabric:

• Cut 4 – 4" x 24¾" outer border strips.

1. With wrong sides together, press each ¾" x 13¼" yellow strip in half lengthwise for the flange. Align the raw edges of two flange strips with raw edges on opposite sides of the quilt center and baste in place. Baste the remaining flange strips to the remaining edges of the quilt center.

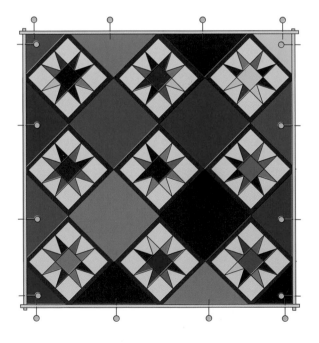

2. With right sides together, pin a 1¼" x 13¼" black inner border strip over the yellow flange strips on the side edges of the quilt center. Sew the inner borders in place, catching the flange pieces in the stitching.

3. Sew the 1¼" x 14¾" black top and bottom inner border strips to the quilt center.

4. Sew the 4" x 24¾" multi-colored outer border strips to the inner border, mitering the corners.

Quilting

For the blocks, I stitched-in-the-ditch around the stars and black sashing pieces and quilted feather designs in the setting pieces and outer border.

Finishing

1. Sew binding to the edges of the quilt.

2. Trim the extra batting and backing, leaving ¼" to ⅜" beyond the quilt top to fill binding. Turn the binding over the edge to the back and hand- or machine-stitch in place.

3. Add a hanging sleeve and label to the quilt back if desired.

Northern Lights Quilting Suggestion

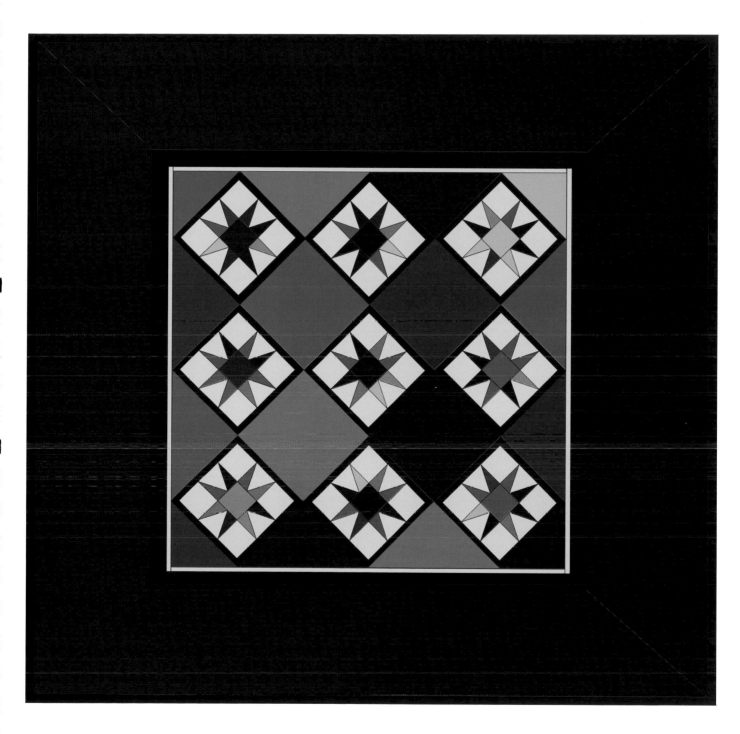

Northern Lights Quilt

summer stars wallhanging

Finished size: 27¼" x 27¼", Block Size: 10"

This wallhanging is simple to make, especially when using the sew-and-flip method on the star points.

fabric requirements

(Based on 42"-wide fabric)

Fat quarter dark pink fabric for inner stars

⅝ yard violet blue fabric for outer star and binding

2 yards light pink fabric for background, sashing, and backing

A piece of batting at least 6" - 8" larger than the quilt top (I used Mountain Mist® Completely Cotton.)

This beautiful table runner will enhance your summer décor. Find complete instructions at www.landauercorp.com

Cutting Instructions

From dark pink fabric:

- Cut 4 – 1¾" x 22" strips.
  From strips cut:
  40 – 1¾" squares

- Cut 5 – 3" squares.

From violet blue fabric:

- Cut 3 – 3" x 42" strips.
  From strips cut:
  32 – 3" squares.

- Cut 2 – 1¾" x 42" strips.
  From strips cut:
  16 – 1¾" squares.
  16 – 1¾" x 3" rectangles.

- Cut 3 – 2½" x 42" binding strips.

From light pink fabric:

- Cut 3 – 3" x 42" strips.
  From strips cut:
  16 – 3" squares.
  4 – 3" x 10½" sashing rectangles.

- Cut 3 – 5½" x 42" strips.
  From strips cut:
  16 – 3" x 5½" rectangles.

Note: Remaining light pink fabric will be cut in Adding the Border.

Making the Star Points

Note: I used the sew-and-flip method to make the star points and sashing strips in this quilt.

1. Draw a diagonal line across the center of all 1¾" dark pink squares and all 3" violet blue squares.

2. With right sides together, lay a 1¾" dark pink square on one end of a 1¾" x 3" violet blue rectangle. Sew on the drawn line.

117

3. Flip the top half of the dark pink square down along the stitching line, and press. Trim only the the bottom half of the dark pink square to ¼".

4. In the same manner, lay a second 1¾" dark pink square on the opposite end of the same violet blue rectangle, so that the diagonal line intersects with the previously sewn line near the center bottom of the rectangle. Sew on the drawn line. Flip the dark pink triangle down and press. As before, trim the bottom half of the dark pink square to ¼" from the seam. Repeat steps 2 through 4 for the remaining 1¾" x 3" violet blue rectangles and 30 – 1¾" dark pink squares to make a total of 16 dark pink star point units.

5. Repeat steps 2 through 4 with the 3" x 5½" light pink rectangles and the 3" violet blue squares, for a total of 16 violet blue star point units.

Make 16

Assembling the Blocks

1. Sew together 4 dark pink star point units, 4 – 1¾" violet blue squares, and 1 – 3" dark pink center square as shown in the diagram.

2. Add 4 violet blue star point units and 4 – 3" light pink corner squares to complete the block. Repeat steps 1 and 2 to make 4 Summer Star blocks. Press the completed block. Make 4 Summer Star blocks.

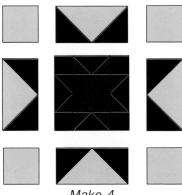

Make 4

Making the Sashing Strips

Sew the remaining 8 – 1¾" dark pink squares to the corners at one end of each of the 4 – 3" x 10½" sashing strips as shown in steps 2 through 4 in Making the Star Points.

Make 4

Assembling the Quilt Center

1. Lay out the 4 Summer Star blocks and the 4 sashing strips, with a 3" dark pink square at the center.

2. Sew together the blocks and sashing strips in rows. Press. Sew the rows together and press. Press the completed quilt center.

Adding the Border

Note: The border measurements are based on the quilt center measuring 23" x 23". If your quilt center measures differently, adjust your border lengths.

From the light pink fabric:

• Cut 2 – 2½" x 23" side border strips.

• Cut 2 – 2½" x 27" top and bottom border strips.

1. Sew the 23" side border strips to the quilt center.

2. Sew the 27" top and bottom strips to the quilt center.

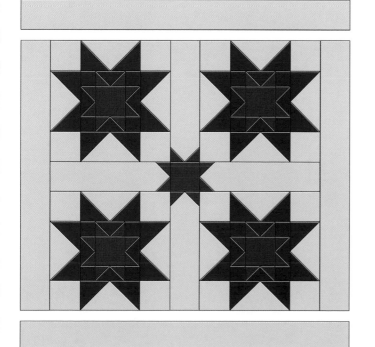

Quilting

I stitched in the ditch around the stars and used echo quilting in the violet blue stars. I quilted a feather wreath in the star centers and free-form feather designs in the pink background.

Finishing

1. Sew binding to the edges of the quilt.

2. Trim the extra batting and backing, leaving ¼" to ⅜" beyond the quilt top to fill binding. Turn the binding over the edge to the back and hand- or machine-stitch in place.

3. Add a hanging sleeve and label to the backing of the quilt, if desired.

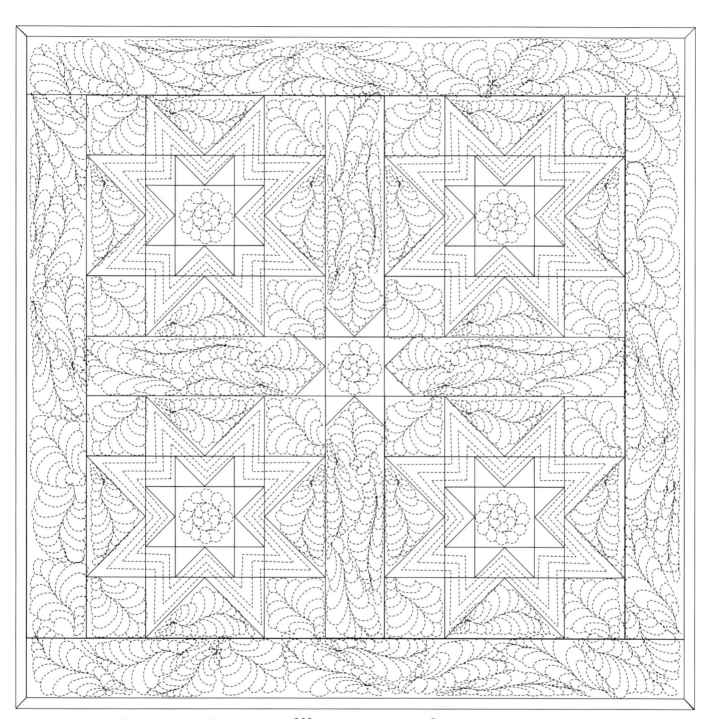

Summer Stars Wallhanging Quilting Suggestion

Summer Stars Wallhanging

scrappy log cabin quilt

Finished Quilt Size: 48½" x 62", Block Size: 6¾"

This quilt is a traditional Log Cabin design made from a pattern shared with many by JoAnn Belling. She shared with our guild that she keeps a collection of pre-cut "logs" on hand at all times. As she purchases new fabrics, she cuts a 1¼" strip from each one, sub-cuts them into various lengths, and stores them with all the other pre-cut logs. Whenever she's ready to do some simple piecing, the cutting is already done. By adopting this habit, the way I did, you'll enjoy making many beautiful log cabin quilts.

fabric requirements

(Based on 42"-wide fabric)

Several 1¼"-wide strips from red fabrics for center squares

1¼"-wide strips from a variety of dark and light fabrics

3 yards backing fabric

½ yard black print fabric for binding

A piece of batting at least 6" - 8" larger than the quilt top (I used Warm & Natural® cotton batting.)

Cutting Instructions

From red 1¼"-wide strips:
- Cut 48 – 1¼" A squares.

Note: Label your strips as you cut to keep them in the correct piecing order.

From light 1¼"-wide fabric strips:
- Cut 48 – 1¼" B squares.
- Cut 48 – 1¼" x 2" C strips.
- Cut 48 – 1¼" x 2¾" F strips.
- Cut 48 – 1¼" x 3½" G strips.
- Cut 48 – 1¼" x 4¼" J strips.
- Cut 48 – 1¼" x 5" K strips.
- Cut 48 – 1¼" x 5¾" N strips.
- Cut 48 – 1¼" x 6½" O strips.

From dark 1¼"-wide fabric strips:
- Cut 48 – 1¼" x 2" D strips.
- Cut 48 – 1¼" x 2¾" E strips.
- Cut 48 – 1¼" x 3½" H strips.
- Cut 48 – 1¼" x 4¼" I strips.
- Cut 48 – 1¼" x 5" L strips.
- Cut 48 – 1¼" x 5¾" M strips.
- Cut 48 – 1¼" x 6½" P strips.
- Cut 48 – 1¼" x 7¼" Q strips.

From black print fabric:
- Cut 6 – 2½" x 42" binding strips.

Note: Making this block will show you right away if your machine's ¼" seam is accurate. If it isn't precisely right, the next "log" won't fit exactly. As with most patchwork, there is a bit of wiggle room in this pattern, but it's best to be as accurate as possible with every seam right from the beginning. Sew a test seam with scrap fabrics and measure your seam allowance width. If it isn't correct, make the necessary adjustments.

Piecing the Log Cabin Blocks

1. Sew the pieces for the Log Cabin block together in alphabetical order, working out counter-clockwise from the center according to the block diagram. Press the seam allowances away from the center A square after sewing each seam. Make 48 Log Cabin blocks.

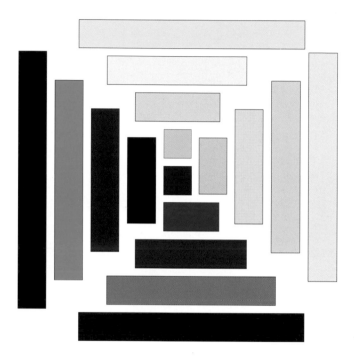

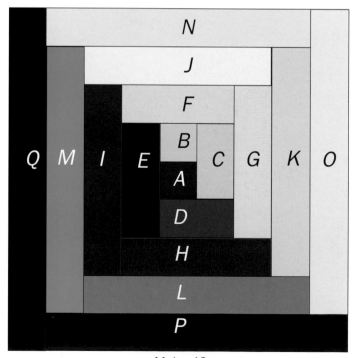

Make 48

Note: There are many different ways to set Log Cabin blocks. I prefer this configuration as it allows for quilting in the lighter areas of the blocks.

Assembling the Quilt Center

1. Lay the blocks out on a flat surface and stitch them into horizontal rows. Press the seams in the same direction within a row and alternate that direction from row to row.

2. Sew the rows together, pressing the seams in the same direction. Press the completed quilt, making sure it lies flat.

Adding the Border

Note: The following measurements are based on the assembled quilt center measuring 41" x 54½". Adjust the length of your border strips if your quilt center measures differently.

1. From border fabric, cut 6 – 4¼" x 42" strips.

2. Stitch 2 sets of 3 strips, using diagonal seams. Press the seam allowances open.

3. From one strip set, cut 2 – 54½" lengths. Sew strips to the sides of the quilt center. Press the seams toward the borders.

4. From the remaining strip set, cut 2 – 48½" lengths. Sew strips to the top and bottom of the quilt center. Press the seams toward the borders.

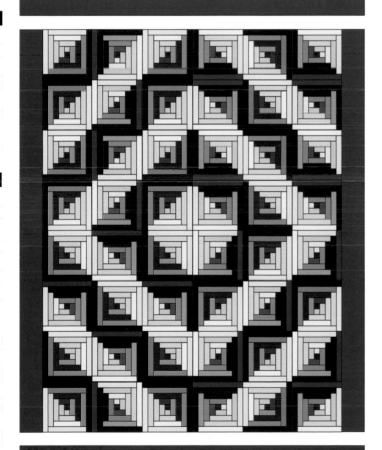

Quilting

Many people have asked me which quilting design I prefer when finishing a log cabin quilt. Since I love feathers, I typically use a feather border design in the lighter areas. In Scrappy Log Cabin, I used a new quilting design from Sherrie Silber. Refer to pages 139-141 for the design. In the darker areas, I stitched in the ditch around each of the 'logs'.

Finishing

1. Sew binding to the edges of the quilt.

2. Trim the extra batting and backing, leaving ¼" to ⅜" beyond the quilt top to fill binding. Turn the binding over the edge to the back and hand- or machine-stitch in place.

3. Add a label to the back of the quilt, if desired.

Scrappy Log Cabin Quilting Suggestion
(See page 139-141 for stencil designs)

Scrappy Log Cabin Quilt

four-patch squared quilt

Finished Quilt Size: 57" x 85½", Block Size: 10"

You'll love making this easy-to-piece, classically beautiful quilt. It's versatile enough to go with any décor depending on how you choose to combine colors. It also leaves plenty of room for great quilting designs.

fabric requirements

(Based on 42"-wide fabric)

16 – 22 light fat quarters

12 – 15 dark fat quarters

5 yards of backing fabric

¾ yards dark green fabric for binding

A piece of batting at least 6" - 8" larger than the quilt top (I used Mountain Mist® Completely Cotton.)

Cutting

From the light fat quarters:

• Cut 60 – 5½" squares.

• Cut 64 – 3" x 10" strips.

• Cut 4 – 15⅜" squares. Cut squares diagonally in both directions to make 16 setting triangles.

• Cut 2 – 8" squares. Cut squares in half diagonally to make 4 corner triangles.

From the dark fat quarters:

• Cut 64 – 3" x 10" strips.

From dark green fabric:

• Cut 7 – 2½" x 42" binding strips.

Making the 16-Patch Blocks

1. Sew the long edges of 1 light and 1 dark 3" x 10" strip together to make a strip set. Repeat to make 64 strip sets. Press the seam allowances toward the dark fabric.

Make 64

2. Cut 3 – 3"-wide segments from each strip set for a total of 192 segments.

Make 192

3. Sew the segments together in pairs, alternating lights and darks, to make 96 – 4-patches.

Make 96

4. Sew the 4-patches together in groups of 4 to make 24 – 16-Patch blocks, being careful to alternate lights and darks each time.

Make 24

Making the 4-Patch Blocks

1. Sew the 5½" squares of light fabric together in pairs. Sew the pairs together in sets of 2 to make 15 – 4-patch blocks.

Make 15

Assembling the Quilt Top

1. Lay the blocks out in diagonal rows, alternating 4-patch blocks with 16-patch blocks. Lay setting triangles at the end of the rows and corner triangles at the 4 corners.

2. Stitch the blocks together into rows, pressing the seam allowances in the same direction within each row, but alternating directions from row to row. Sew the rows together and press the completed quilt top.

Quilting

I quilted this quilt with feather designs in the blocks. See if you can come up with some other creative ideas of your own.

Finishing

1. Sew binding to the edges of the quilt.

2. Trim the extra batting and backing, leaving ¼" to ³⁄₈" beyond the quilt top to fill binding. Turn the binding over the edge to the back and hand- or machine-stitch in place.

3. Add a hanging sleeve and label to the quilt back, if desired.

Four-patch squared stencil design
Enlarge 120% to equal approximately 10"

Four-Patch Squared Quilting Suggestion

Four-Patch Squared Quilt

Block
Stencils

Enlarge or reduce
the stencils
to fit your project

Sashing Stencil

Enlarge or reduce
the stencils
to fit your project

Stencils for Dashes of Color Quilt (page 94)

Block Stencil

*Enlarge or reduce
the stencils
to fit your project*

Corner & Border Stencil

*Enlarge or reduce
the stencils
to fit your project*

Triangle Stencil

Enlarge or reduce the stencils to fit your project

Border
Stencil

*Enlarge or reduce
the stencils
to fit your project*

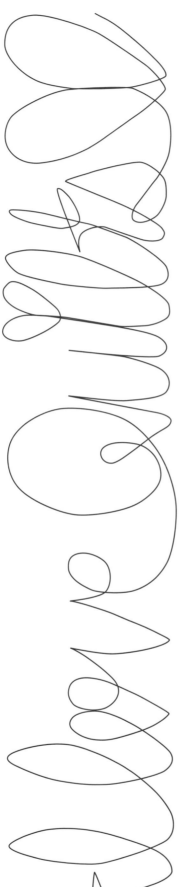

Corner
Option

*Enlarge or reduce
the stencils
to fit your project*

Corner
Option

*Enlarge or reduce
the stencils
to fit your project*

Stencil for I Love Quilts (page 104)

Triangle Stencil

*Enlarge or reduce
the stencils
to fit your project*

Block Stencil

*Enlarge or reduce
the stencils
to fit your project*

Border Stencil

*Enlarge or reduce
the stencils
to fit your project*

Stencil for Scrappy Log Cabin Quilt (page 122)

Corner
&
Border
Stencil

Enlarge or reduce
the stencils
to fit your project

Stencil for Scrappy Log Cabin Quilt (page 122)

Block Stencil

*Enlarge or reduce
the stencils
to fit your project*

Triangle Stencil

*Enlarge or reduce
the stencils
to fit your project*

Bonus—Apple Blossom Stencils

Border Stencil

Enlarge or reduce the stencils to fit your project

Bonus—Apple Blossom Stencils

Resources

Beeline+Blue
2507 Ingersoll Avenue
Des Moines, IA 50312
(800) 347-1610
www.beelineandblue.com

Creekside Quilting
9926 Swanson Blvd.
Clive, IA 50325
(515) 276-1977
www.creekside-quilting.com

Golden Threads
245 W. Roosevelt Rd.
Suite 61
West Chicago, IL 60185
(888) 477-7718
www.goldenthreads.com

JoAnn Belling
4008 156th Street
Des Moines, IA 50323
(515) 987-4912
www.joannbelling.com

Hobbs Bonded Fibers
200 South Commerce Dr.
Waco, Texas 76710
(254) 741-0040
www.hobbsbondedfibers.com

Mountain Mist
2551 Crescentville Road
Cincinnati, OH 45241
(800) 345-7150
www.mountainmistlp.com

Quilting Creations
PO Box 512
Zoar, OH 44697
(877) 219-9899
www.quilting creations.com

Quilters Dream Batting
589 Central Drive,
Virginia Beach, VA 23454
(888) 268-8664
www.quiltersdreambatting.com

Robert Kaufman Co., Inc.
129 West 132nd Street
Los Angeles, CA 90061
(800) 877-2066
www.robertkaufman.com

Sherrie Silber
4708 South Arthur Circle
Sioux Falls, SD 57105
s.silber@yahoo.com

Sulky® of America
900 Cobb Place Blvd., Ste. 130
Kennesaw, GA 30144
(800) 874-4115
www.sulky.com

Superior Threads
87 East 2580 South
St. George, UT 84790
(800) 499-1777
www.superiorthreads.com

The Kansas City Star
1729 Grand Blvd.
Kansas City, MO 64108
For more information about
the history of the Kansas City Star
quilt patterns, visit the Kansas City Star
Quilts web site at www.PickleDish.com.

The Stencil Company
28 Castlewood Dr., Dept. WW
Cheektowaga, NY 14227
(716) 656-9430
www.quiltingstencils.com

The Warm Company,
5529 186th Place SW,
Lynnwood, Washington, 98037
(425) 248-2424
www.warmcompany.com

Special thanks to…
Connie Doern at Creekside Quilting for supplying a sewing machine
and notions for photography and for allowing us to take over her classroom for a few photos.

Robert Kaufman, Inc. for supplying the Kona® cotton fabrics shown in the how-to chapters.